The Pure love

A tragic romance, set in
Islamic society during
the gunmrn's occupation
of Mosul
A Novel
Arshad Rashid Al-Hamdany
2024

The Pure Love

Arshad Al-Hamdani

Published by Arshad Al-Hamdani, 2024.

While every precaution has been taken in the preparation of this book, the publisher assumes no responsibility for errors or omissions, or for damages resulting from the use of the information contained herein.

THE PURE LOVE

First edition. June 11, 2024.

ISBN: 979-8227242471

Written by Arshad Al-Hamdani.

CONTENT

Author's notes

The novel "The Pure Love" is a new version of "Fouad and Layla." It delves into the heartfelt love story of Fouad and Layla amidst the backdrop of the gunmen's reign over Mosul. The narrative unfolds against the backdrop of various events that transpired within the city, including the harrowing exodus of its inhabitants before, during, and after the militant group's control. Additionally, the novel offers a poignant portrayal of the daily struggles faced by individuals living under the oppressive rule of the militants.

All names in this work are symbolic rather than real, and locations are intentionally vague to avoid any direct references to actual individuals.

Readers of this work experience the suffering of the city's inhabitants before, during, and after armed individuals took over the city.

1
She Accidentally Pierced His Heart with an Arrow

In his final year of high school, Fouad, an eighteen-year-old, stands out as a strikingly tall individual with dark brown hair, hazel eyes, and a full beard. Though he can be bashful around girls and women, he is a bright and pious young man. He shines as the standout player on the school's volleyball team, admired by his peers for his unwavering moral values, upbeat personality, and talent for spreading joy with his humor. Both on and off the court, his leadership and optimistic outlook set him apart as a remarkable student-athlete.

Despite his popularity, Fouad remains modest and respectful toward women. He tries hard not to look at girls when he sees them, whether at school or elsewhere. While he may catch a glimpse of a female entering or leaving a neighbor's house, he refrains from turning his head to look at her.

In Iraqi culture, it is customary for families to share a portion of their delicious meals with neighbors. Typically, the recipient returns the container filled rather than empty, keeping it if they have nothing valuable to offer. Moreover, when they prepare a delicious dish, they portion some of it into a container and pass it back to the neighbor once more.

Fouad's mother, Khadija, is a delightful and humble gynecologist with a great sense of humor, both at home and in her professional life. She asks Fouad to answer the door whenever the doorbell rings; however, Fouad has a unique response each time, saying, "Please go ahead, Mother. With all due respect, the person at the door could be a girl or a woman. Therefore, I am unable to engage in any conversation with them."

One day, when the doorbell rang, Fouad found himself alone in the house. Reluctantly, he went to answer and was surprised to encounter a veiled girl standing there holding a plate of candy. She wore a stylish black scarf that accentuated her beauty, and her face radiated like the moon on a dark night. Their eyes met briefly, and it seemed as though she had cast a spell on him, capturing his heart in that moment.

Since he did not know her, he waited for a moment to see which house she entered in order to return the plate to her. He realized she had entered the right-side neighbor's house.

He returned, positioned the dish in the kitchen, and took a small bite of that delectable food before returning to his room.

He frequently consumed this kind of sweet but had never had this pleasant flavor before; therefore, he would occasionally go back and nibble on a small amount until he had consumed half of that sweet.

She realized that she captivated Fouad, from his gaze towards her to his confusion. His striking good looks, impressive stature, strong moral character, and respectful demeanor toward women left a lasting impression on her. She couldn't help but notice his reluctance to make eye contact with girls as she passed by. Many women admire a man who doesn't chase after girls with his gaze.

He brought his book to study, determined to focus solely on his education during this critical time. However, a persistent, strange feeling continued to nag at him, making it difficult to concentrate.

When the doorbell rang on the second day, his mother was ready to answer it, anticipating that Fouad would come up with an excuse. However, to her surprise, Fouad rose from his seat and made his way to the door without hesitation. It was then that he realized he was an electrical meter reader.

"It's not your usual practice to open the door. What inspired this behavior?" His mother asked and smiled.

"Now, every young person reaches a turning point in his development when he becomes spiritually mature, feels responsible, and recognizes his parental duties. So I won't let you get tired anymore," he replied with a laugh, shaking his head.

"Bravo, Fouad, bravo. My efforts in raising you have not been in vain," she stated proudly.

Fouad had strong motivation to open the door whenever the bell rang. Every time he went to open it, he met someone else. He also does not want to stand in her way when she is going to or coming back from school, as he considers this to be a sin and damaging to his reputation and that of his family. This behavior towards the neighbors is considered unethical.

He said to his mother a few days later, "Mom, our neighbor has an empty dish that we have to return with some delicious food or sweets."

"Sure, I'll get right on that tomorrow," she replied with a hint of surprise.

Fouad seems to be getting more and more impatient, acting like tomorrow is light years away. The following day, his mother lovingly whipped up a delicious meal and shared some with their neighbor.

"Oh, Mother, I simply can't bear to see you bear yourself out like this. Let me take that dish off your hands," Fouad declared as he reached for the plate.

He rang the doorbell and waited anxiously. When her father, Othman, answered the door, Fouad greeted him warmly and handed over the food before departing, feeling disheartened. As he walked away, Fouad couldn't shake the feeling of disappointment.

He conversed with himself while alone at night, reflected on his emotions, and attributed his behavior to the devil's inclination. He subsequently resolved to place the incident in the past and concentrate on his studies, as he had reached a critical juncture.

Two weeks later, after the bell sounded, Fouad just felt that he was opening the door when, all of a sudden, his eyes caught hers. He felt as though an arrow had just pierced his heart, but he was able to control himself. He accepted the dish, nodded, and smiled as he expressed his gratitude for her.

Never before had he experienced such comfort, but he tried to neglect the situation and concentrate on his studies.

A month later, while walking, he noticed her returning from school. His thoughts raced as he concentrated on her stunning features and penetrating stare. He closed his eyes, rubbed his hair, and thought as he walked. The abrupt honking of a vehicle caught him off guard, prompting him to swiftly scan his surroundings and discover he was in the center of the road. Acting without delay, he dashed towards the sidewalk.

As he sat in the classroom, it was clear that his thoughts were elsewhere, completely detached from the lesson at hand. Despite his best efforts to reign in his wandering mind, it seemed determined to stray. The teacher observed Fouad's lack of focus and inability to concentrate, which was a stark contrast to his typically engaged and well-behaved behavior.

"Fouad, do enlighten us on where we currently stand in this lesson." The teacher inquired

Fouad flinched, meeting the teacher's gaze sheepishly before responding, "Oh, my apologies, dear teacher."

The teacher raised an eyebrow, patience wearing thin. "Perhaps you could grace us with a summary of my previous words?" he suggested.

"Sorry, sir, I was distracted." He admitted

As the teacher stood before the class, a brave soul dared to speak up, proclaiming, "It seems that Fouad has found himself smitten!" The room erupted in laughter, causing poor Fouad's cheeks to flush with embarrassment. He regretted his romantic entanglement and the public humiliation it brought upon him. The teacher, in a tone dripping with sarcasm, scolded the unruly students for their lack of empathy and assured Fouad that he could help him if he needed it.

Oh, the drama of young love! Put him in an awkward position.

Fouad expressed his gratitude to the teacher and clarified that he was dealing with a temporary personal matter.

Later that evening, he found himself alone, engaging in self-reflection and having a stern conversation with himself. He attributed it to the devil's attempt to sabotage his life and thwart his future. How convenient. "Regardless of the result, I suppose I should probably end this behavior, no matter how much of a hassle it may be."

For over a month, he stubbornly clung to his decision. When his mother requested his help opening the door or running errands for their neighbors, his excuse was always the same: "Sorry, Mom, but I have an exam to study for." He used to see her going to or coming back from school, but he decided not to lift his gaze to look at her. He saw it as resisting the devil's temptation, and he prided himself on his unwavering determination.

Fouad's mother was ill. Layla and her mother visited their neighbor because, as is customary in Iraq, the neighbors go to each other and bring gifts when they visit the sick.

Layla rang the doorbell, holding a gift in her hand, but there was no one to answer except Fouad, who graciously welcomed them inside. Layla's mother exchanged greetings with Fouad before entering the house, followed by Layla, who also greeted him. As Layla presented him with the gift, Fouad extended his hand to receive it without even looking at her. However, just as he was about to take hold of the gift, Layla intentionally let it slip from her grasp. The chocolates scattered upon impact, and the gift tumbled to the floor. "How clever are the girls! They always seem to find creative solutions to any problem thrown their way."

Overwhelmed by embarrassment, he picked up the chocolates from the floor and expressed his deep remorse. Layla and her mother helped him collect the chocolates.

"I must offer my sincerest apologies, for it appears that I have committed a grave error by allowing the gift to slip through my fingers before you could catch it," Layla confessed, attempting to alleviate the awkwardness of the situation.

Layla and her mother joined Fouad's mother for a visit. Fouad found himself the soul caretaker of the guests because of his mother's health issue; as part of his duties, he provided them with water, tea, coffee, and pastries, all while maintaining a cheerful demeanor and making sure to keep eye contact with her to avoid any further mishaps, like one that happened at the door.

"I deeply regret the unfortunate incident at the door," he apologized. Confusion arose when his mother inquired about the incident, prompting Fouad to recount the entire embarrassing ordeal. Much to his surprise, his mother found the situation amusing, leading to a round of laughter from everyone present.

After spending about an hour together, Layla and her mother decided it was time to leave. Fouad's mother called out for him to escort them to the door, bidding them a heartfelt farewell.

Fouad started living a contradictory life; although his will and reason stopped him from acting on his desires, his feelings pulled him toward her. Although his feelings for her returned strongly, she bewitched him with her charming eyes. He decided to withstand and resist indifference, and he addressed himself, saying, "This is a test of your willpower, Fouad."

One day, when Layla's mother turned on the cooker to begin preparing supper, she noticed that the natural gas cylinder was empty. She had bought an unused cylinder a few days earlier, but when she went to bring it, she discovered that it was empty since there had been an infrequent gas leak from the valve.

She pressed her neighbor's doorbell. Fouad opened the door; no one else was in the house. After explaining the situation, Layla's mother requested a replacement cylinder of natural gas and assured him that she would return another one once she replaced the current one. In response, he said that this was the neighbor's binding duty and then brought the gas cylinder.

Despite Layla's mother's interest in taking the bottle from him, he refused, stating that it would not be honorable to have her carry the heavy cylinder. "This is too much for you," he said.

He confidently walked towards the kitchen, feeling the strain of the heavy cylinder on his muscles. Meanwhile, Layla was engrossed in washing dishes, oblivious to his arrival. Suddenly, he let out a loud cough, almost as if to signal his presence—a custom apparently observed in Iraqi society. Startled by the unexpected noise, Layla turned around to see him walking toward the kitchen, a small smile playing on his lips.

Upon hearing his cough, Layla swiftly adjusted her attire, draping a sleek black scarf to cover her hair and around her neck and smoothing out her sleeves. She stood poised, anticipating his entrance.

As he entered the room, his eyes met hers, and he greeted her with a warm hello. Layla responded with a shy smile; her cheeks turned red with a hint of color.

As his heart raced, he dramatically declared, "I shall expertly place the cylinder in its designated spot, as this task is clearly too challenging for you to handle." In a comical turn of events, Fouad struggled to remove the old cylinder from its cramped location and ended up cutting his finger on the sink's sharp edge. Blood gushed out, prompting Layla to start wailing in horror. She quickly fetched the sterilizer and instant dressing, all while apologizing profusely. She courageously stated, "I would prefer to have the injury on my finger than to witness you in pain."

Upon hearing Layla's words, he momentarily forgot about his wound and the pain he was enduring. Following Layla's mother's care of Fouad's injury, he managed to effectively install the cylinder; once he finished the task, he emerged from the kitchen and proceeded to the outdoor entrance, where she followed him to slam the door. She overheard him humming the poetry of the hermit 'Amer ibn Abi Rabee'ah, and he was unaware that she was walking behind him.

Tell Maliha with the black veil. What have you done to a worshipful hermit? Who had rolled up his clothes for prayer until you stood next to him at the mosque outlet?

She was filled with overwhelming joy upon hearing those words, convinced that he was referring to her in the hymn. This was the most beautiful song she had ever heard, and she found herself humming it to herself from time to time, feeling immense joy when she did.

I wish the wound was on my finger, not yours. Its echo reverberates in his ears. Since he heard those words, he couldn't stop thinking about her.

One day, as he was engrossed in his studies, the doorbell suddenly rang, jolting him out of his concentration. Without realizing it, he found himself standing at the door, ready to greet whoever was on the other side. His heartbeat raced as soon as he caught a glimpse of her eyes. Her piercing eyes shot out an arrow, sending his entire body shaking. In his expression of appreciation, he remarked, "Your cookery is exquisite; I have never tasted anything comparable, and you are the most beautiful young lady on the planet."

She smiled silently, leaving him feeling regretful and bewildered. He had no idea how the words had come out of his tongue. Fouad found he was unable to resist the urge to see her; his desire was growing uncontrollable. He knew he was in love and powerless to stop it. Realizing that his conflicting emotions were hindering his studies, he reluctantly confided in his mother.

"I want to marry Layla," the son declared.

"Son, as you approach the end of your academic journey, it is crucial that you focus on your education full-time. It would be wise to wait until after you have completed your studies before considering marriage."

"I find it difficult to focus on my studies unless I complete her betrothal," the son forcefully retorted.

"Please discuss this issue with your father. I doubt he will agree," his mother said.

During the dinner, Fouad's mother casually dropped a bombshell, saying, "Tell your father about it."

Fouad was startled. "Tell him about what?" he asked.

"You know it—the thing you told me yesterday. Spit it out; don't be shy." She replied,

"What's going on?" His father inquired, sensing the tension.

After mustering up the courage, he finally confessed, "I am deeply in love with Layla, and I want to spend the rest of my life with her. She consumes my thoughts, and I cannot imagine my future without her by my side. She has me completely enamored, and I can't stop thinking about her."

His father, clearly annoyed, asked, "Have you really thought this through, or is it just a passing fancy?"

Fouad, determined, replied, "I've thought long and hard about it."

His father, still skeptical, questioned, "And does Layla even know about this plan?"

Fouad sheepishly admitted, "I'm not sure, but you can talk to her father and find out."

"Remove this idea completely from your mind before finishing your studies, and then talk about it later. And then for every recent event." His father said it with a hint of impatience.

"Dear beloved father, please understand my feelings; I am unable to focus on my studies if I do not complete her engagement." Fouad replied

"I am reiterating my statement for the second time. Please refrain from compelling me to restate it in a more severe tone. Get this idea out of your head before you complete your studies," said his father.

Fouad rose from his seat and politely excused himself before retreating to his room. As he took a small bite of food, his expression twisted with sorrow.

His mother followed him to his room and saw him lying on his bed, almost in tears. She began advising him to postpone this idea until after the exam. She informed him that his father desires what is best for him. Once he completes his studies, they will organize his engagement. Despite this, he remained silent, not uttering a single word as tears started to flow down his cheeks.

Mothers have tender hearts and quickly show compassion towards their sons and daughters. Khadija went to her husband and asked him to fulfill Fouad's wishes, because he was now sad and heartbroken. However, his father remained adamant in his opinion and refused to discuss the matter further.

Several days passed, and Fouad did not attend to the table during meal times. When he did come, he would only eat a bite or two to please his parents and then remain silent without speaking.

One day, three of them sat down for dinner. Fouad ate two bites and stopped. Fouad's mother did not reach for the food and remained still, sadness evident on her face.

"Why aren't you eating?" his father asked, surprised.

She replied, "I won't eat unless you fulfill Fouad's wish and ask for Layla's hand in marriage."

His father's face darkened, and his cheeks puffed out, indicating he wanted to speak. However, he held back his words, left the table, and went to his room. Fouad's mother followed him but found that he had closed the door.

She sat on the sofa in the living room, and the atmosphere of the house suddenly turned gloomy. Fouad's father appeared to have fallen asleep, and after two hours, he opened the door and came out. He sat next to his wife, looking visibly upset. Placing his hand on her back, he began to rub it gently. He apologized for leaving them on the table and storming out angrily, saying, "How can we resolve this issue? The situation at home has turned upside down."

"My belief is that we should start by asking for Layla's hand in marriage because our son does not eat or read; his health will deteriorate, and he will fail in his studies." She replied,

"Alright, you can start making arrangements according to tradition." He ordered.

Fouad's mother paid a visit to Layla's humble abode, graciously informing her mother of her son's desire to take Layla's hand in marriage. Her mother made sure to emphasize that the final decision would be contingent upon Layla's wishes and the approval of her father. Her mother praised his impeccable morals, and she also acknowledged the family's renowned reputation. This behavior demonstrates the girl's engagement in Iraqi culture.

During dinner, her mother set off a bomb in Othman's house. Layla's face lit up when she heard the news, but she remained silent out of respect for her father. However, Layla's father firmly stated that he would not engage in discussing the issue at hand as Layla was on the brink of her final exams, and he believed it would negatively impact her academic performance. But quickly, her expression changed from joy to sadness.

Days later, Layla heard via Fouad's mother that the situation was dire and that the boy was not eating or studying. Layla decided to follow the same path. She sat at the table, refusing to eat and abstaining from studying. Her mother informed her father that the condition of the boy and girl was deteriorating rapidly, emphasizing the importance of fulfilling their wishes.

Layla's father remained stubborn for two weeks, refusing to engage in any discussion on the matter. In the end, Layla's father, Othman, accepted the inevitable.

A few days later, Layla's father, Othman, finally gave his blessing to seal the deal on the engagement, and Layla's mother sent the good news to Fouad's mother.

The tribal sheikh, Dr. Suhail, along with his siblings, journeyed to Othman's residence to attend the grand event. Of course, they didn't forget to bring a lot of chocolate and candies, as sweet days need sweets.

The sheikh buttered up Othman by praising his family's impeccable reputation. Othman, in turn, returned the favor by complimenting Fouad's chivalrous nature and noble morals. So, there you have it: Layla and Fouad are officially on the path to marital bliss.

The wedding will conveniently take place after their final exams, which are about two months away. Layla and Fouad got engaged that evening in accordance with their religious and cultural traditions, and they later signed a formal contract in court to formally consummate their marriage.

They immediately began preparing their house and making plans for the impending nuptials.

But the unthinkable occurred.

2
Suddenly, the City Transformed into a Battlefield

Nearing fifty years old, Satam has been a trader on Mosul's left side. He was an average-statured, chatty, plump man with a large jaw, a harsh voice, and a sense of humor.

His friend Ahmed, a tribe Sheikh, is 57 years old and a tall, lean, charming, intelligent, and well-known man. He has a round beard. He is generous with dignity and a good reputation, and he has been living on the right side of the city.

He has a diwan where visitors, friends, and neighbors regularly congregate. Diwan has an annex that accommodates overnight visitors from outside the city, and there are always visitors. This Diwan serves as a platform for resolving numerous social issues, offering an alternative to traditional court proceedings.

They engage in discussions on a range of topics, including the challenging security environment and the dire living conditions that existed both before and after armed militants seized control of roughly one-third of Iraq's territory.

One day, Satam went to see his friend Ahmed, who greeted him and inquired,

"It's been a while since you haven't visited us."

"Oh, Sheikh," Satam exclaimed, "I am at a loss for words. None of us have the inclination to venture outside our homes, especially considering the current state of Mosul, which resembles a military encampment. The journey to your residence alone involves passing through twelve security checkpoints, each accompanied by extensive car queues. "It is common knowledge that anyone daring to leave their abode will experience significant delays lasting for hours."

"Indeed, you are correct," replied Ahmed. "I recently visited Mosul Municipality just last week. I had departed at 9:50 a.m. with the expectation of arriving by 11:30 a.m. However, upon my arrival at 1:30 p.m., I was disheartened to find that the staff was already preparing to leave."

There was a checkpoint for different security forces belonging to the government every 2000–3000 meters everywhere you travel inside the city, and what makes the crowding much worse is that the checkpoints were located at road intersections, traffic lights, and over bridges.

However, the security situation in Mosul was deteriorating rapidly. Explosions, bomb traps, kidnappings, killings, and beheadings were happening on a daily basis and were growing frighteningly frequent. Additionally, armed gunmen were extorting money from various businesses, pharmacies, and doctors, as well as owners of trucks, buses, and parking facilities. In Mosul, gunmen typically required a 10% share of the contractor's fee as a standard practice for project completion.

Despite these escalating threats, there were no reports of any security checkpoints successfully apprehending any terrorists. The situation was dire; as the saying goes, "The dead are a mouse, and the funeral is large."

Satam requested permission to leave, jokingly adding, "I have to go through 12 checkpoints.

After an explosion rocked his neighborhood three weeks ago, Ahmed asked Satam to join him in visiting their friend Malik the next day. Then, they planned to visit another friend, Ali, whose house was near a recent explosion.

Despite the frequent explosions in the area, social obligations continued without pause.

The following day, they found Malik's house untouched by the blast. After confirming everyone's safety over a cup of coffee, they made their way to Ali's house.

They discovered that Ali's home was close to a recent car explosion at a military barracks on Baghdad Road. The blast violently tore the doors and windows from their frames and caused casualties among civilians and troops. Ali's daughter sustained injuries from shattered glass. Ahmed advised Ali, "It looks like you need some new windows and doors."

"I certainly will," Ali replied.

Satam remarked that the tour in Mosul resembled a visit to an army camp. When they attempted to offer him money, Ali firmly refused. However, they continued to insist, urging him to accept the cash as a gesture of support in dealing with the accident.

Satam frustrated.

Several days later, Satam visited Sheikh Ahmed, expressing his frustration: "I have reached my limit; my mental state is exhausted, and I am unable to sleep at night due to constant worrying."

Worries about potential kidnappings and ransom demands were a constant concern for business owners, medical professionals, high-profile individuals, and affluent residents of Mosul. If the kidnapped person is unable to pay the ransom within the specified time frame, the kidnappers will execute him.

Many professionals, including doctors, professors, and business people, had left the country due to the poor security conditions.

Ahmed encouraged Satam, advising him to prioritize self-care, exercise caution, and embrace the situation before surrendering to fate.

"There isn't a tree that hasn't experienced wind-shaken adversity, and there isn't a man who hasn't faced challenges, but strong trees withstand storms and strong men stand their ground and overcome challenges, so you should be one of them and resist allowing despair to consume you."

Ahmed's doorbell rang as they were talking. When he answered it, his friend Saeed was waiting for him outside. Ahmed ushered him inside the house and gave him a warm welcome. A mixture of restraint and frustration was apparent on Saeed's face.

"Ha! Satam, how are you?" Saeed said,

"Welcome, dear Saeed," Satam replied. "Why do you look so angry?"

"Friends, when I was coming, I saw two beheaded bodies in Al Sawwas's vicinity; with the heads resting on the bodies' backs, I was tempted to walk away in disgust, but I ultimately decided to stay because my desire to be with you outweighed my repulsion." Saeed said it with a tone tinged with impatience.

"These repetitive scenes occur on a weekly basis, causing many individuals to avoid unnecessary walks," Ahmed said, adding, "You can shake off this exhaustion and anxiety by having lunch at the farm tomorrow."

The bell rang again; two hours later, Ahmed came out, and there were a bunch of troops. The officer approached him and informed him that the neighborhood was undergoing a raid to search for firearms. He cautioned him that if he possessed a weapon and failed to surrender it, he would also be subject to arrest.

"I have an old pistol with 20 bullets that I keep for emergency self-defense," said Ahmed.

"Bring the pistol with ammo," the officer ordered.

"I told you that the pistol was for self-defense," Ahmed protested. "If I give it to you, I'll remain unarmed."

"I told you to bring the pistol. Don't make us late for our duty; otherwise, we will arrest you," the officer replied.

Ahmed retrieved the weapon from the hidden stash in the bunker, which had eluded detection by the military group despite their thorough search. He then handed it over to the officer, along with the rounds. The officer accepted the weapon and directed it towards Ahmed's neighbors.

Satam became enraged when Ahmed handed them the weapon and said it clearly.

"Why did you tell them that you have a weapon? They couldn't discover it, no matter how thoroughly they searched the house."

"I was afraid that the officer would see you in my house and ask, why are you gathered here? And what are you doing? So I gave up the weapon to save you."

The authorities not only seized Ahmed's weapons but also took further action." The army and other security forces conducted multiple raids on homes in Mosul city and its outskirts, seizing any firearms discovered.

Satam's shoulders heaved suddenly as tears streamed down his face, causing Ahmed to inquire about the source of his distress. However, Satam was unable to speak through his sobs.

After composing himself, Satam finally managed to explain, " I remembered my Christian friend, Jarjees, and his family " He paused, taking a deep breath before continuing, "When armed men forced them to leave the city, my family and I went to their home to say goodbye. It was a heartbreaking scene. I extended an offer of financial assistance and any other support I could provide, but Jarjees declined, expressing concern for their safety in light of their possessions.

Tears welled up in Satam's eyes as he recounted, "I watched as my young daughter hugged their child, begging her to stay. And then, as they left, I saw one of the armed men snatch a golden necklace from a woman." Satam sighed heavily, admitting, "I underestimated my own value in that moment."

The emotional turmoil of witnessing his friend's family being forced to leave and the realization of his own vulnerability left Satam shaken.

Fish Feast on the Farm

Ahmed owns a sprawling farm with trees, a lavish mansion, a garden, and vast fields of wheat and barley on the city outskirts.

On the second day, Ahmed, Satam, Saeed, a guest from Baghdad, and a group of other friends visited Ahmed's farm. The wheat and barley fields, along with the grasslands, are dyed in their green attire, adorned with various colors of flowers, in a sight that refreshes the soul and soothes the heart, as far as the eye could see.

They sat in the garden, shielded from the rain, and marveled at the sun's golden rays peering through the scattered clouds and the rainbow's arc of brilliant colors stretching over the horizon. This happened after a brief downpour of rain.

In addition to preparing the salad and snacks he brought from the city, Ahmed requested that the guard catch many fish from the fish farming pond and grill them over firewood, and he directed him to cook them on low heat.

They rose for the midday prayer, and Sheikh Rifaat led them in prayer as an imam. Following their prayer, Satam began cracking jokes to lighten the mood and distract them from the melancholy they were experiencing in the city.

Two hours later, the guard arrived with bread, salad, and grilled fish. He set everything out on the table, and everyone began to eat.

They heard sounds of multiple pickups stopping abruptly, and guys with guns came out and surrounded the area.

Ahmed requested that everyone remain seated so that he could bargain with them. The guards proceeded to the guard room, retrieved their weapons, and positioned themselves inside to respond to any potential issues. Ahmed instructed Satam to join them in the guard room, arm himself, and take charge of directing the guards in case of an emergency.

What do you want?" Ahmed inquired as he neared the group.

The commander of the gunmen declared, "There is a police officer among you."

Ahmed quickly responded, "There are no policemen among us; we are all civilians."

The commander stated, "We have information that there is a police officer among you."

"That's not accurate," he retorted.

"We need to verify your identities," the commander stated.

"It is unacceptable for you to inquire about someone's identification; these are my guests. Ahmed yelled, "Shame on you; you're all younger than my son!" with a fiery tone.

"We have to search everyone," their leader yelled. Voices became more audible between them and Ahmed. He alternates between severity and calmness because he fears they may return and harm the guards later on. When the guest from Baghdad discovered that they were interested in confirming everyone's identification,

"It's no problem; they can verify our identities instead of being a mishap," the guest from Baghdad commented.

Ahmed refused to allow them to search his guests, and the situation escalated to a threat of using weapons. The guest arrived and pleaded with Ahmed to allow them to search before things took a turn for the worse.

"You don't enter the farm, but I will bring the identities to you," stated Ahmed.

The gunmen carefully surveyed the identification cards to ensure there were no police officers among them, retreating once Ahmed presented the cards of everyone.

"What are their demands from the police?" The visitor from Baghdad asked

"Gunmen militants have ruthlessly and senselessly claimed the lives of policemen, soldiers, government officials, and politicians," Ahmed lamented. "Unfortunately, thousands of police officers and army personnel from Mosul and its surrounding areas have lost their lives in the line of duty. This has created a climate of fear among those who continue to serve, with many too terrified to even report for work. Many people resigned from their positions out of fear for their safety and lives." Despite the significant military presence in the city, the army has been unable to prevent terrorists from targeting and killing both its own members and civilians.

On The Morning Of June 10, 2014

Satam eagerly waited for the stunning red twilight that would emerge after the Fajr prayer, just before sunrise, while enjoying a steaming cup of coffee on his rooftop on the morning of June 10th. This daily ritual brought him immense joy and tranquility.

Suddenly and without warning, the right side of the city of Mosul erupted into a battlefield with sporadic gunfire. Two days later, the action shifted from the right side of the city to the left side without any resistance from the military or other official armed factions.

Satam contacted Ahmed and inquired about the cause of the sporadic explosions, their location, and whether they were safe.

Ahmed and the other residents found themselves trapped in their homes on the right side of the city, surrounded by gunfire and shells. They were unable to leave their homes and were oblivious to the developing situation, according to Ahmed.

Ramus, a middle-aged math teacher of short stature, resides in the Danadan neighborhood near Mosul's Fourth Bridge. Three days after the armed forces took control of the city, he decided to visit his son, who lives near Ahmed's house.

After ensuring the safety of his son and family, Rami paid a visit to his acquaintance, Ahmed. Upon his arrival, Ahmed warmly greeted him and exclaimed, "The blessing has visited us!" He graciously invited him inside.

Rami apologized to Ahmed, explaining that he had only come to inquire at the door and planned to return promptly due to the unstable situation. The city was on edge as the gunmen responsible for recent events remained unknown, causing fear among residents who were hesitant to leave their homes unless necessary.

Despite Rami's insistence on leaving quickly, Ahmed refused to let him go without first sharing a meal. As they sat down to eat, they began discussing the recent events that took place in the city.

"Sheikh Ahmed, do you know who these gunmen are?"

"No one knows them yet, but I heard that these are clan revolutionaries and former officers, but it lacks confirmation."

Initially, there were allegations that the gunmen involved in the incident were retired army officers and members of a tribe engaged in a revolution. However, they did not reveal their identities until they had fully taken control of the city.

Initially, flags representing various factions were present but eventually disappeared.

Rami noted a peculiar observation that left him puzzled, stating the following:

"I saw a strange thing that made my mind stop thinking, and I couldn't find an explanation."

"What was that?" asked Ahmed.

"My house is located near the fourth bridge," Rami explained. "On the day militants entered the city, I climbed onto the roof and observed a peculiar scene unfolding below. Two pickup trucks, each armed with a single anti-aircraft weapon and manned by gunmen, stood at the entrance of the bridge from the Dawwasa side. "In between them were thousands of army members escaping, some fleeing in military vehicles, others on foot, dressed in a mix of military uniforms and civilian clothing." As Rami continued, he described the tense standoff he witnessed. "Despite the proximity between the escaping soldiers and the gunmen, neither side made a move against the other. The lack of conflict between them made me bewildered and intrigued by the unusual situation."

"I have also heard the same," Ahmed agreed. Reports indicate that only three hundred militants armed with light and medium weapons infiltrated Mosul."" With a look of disbelief, he continued, "The government's formidable army, consisting of approximately 100,000 well-equipped soldiers, possessed a vast array of heavy, light, and medium weaponry, in addition to four helicopters. It is truly baffling how they abandoned their arms and retreated, leaving behind such a substantial arsenal."

"With time, things will become clear," Rami said. "Things will unfold in the future. But I'm worried; my heart is racing, and our future remains unknown and terrifying."

3
Oh, Unfulfilled Joy

Several months after the gunmen seized control of Mosul, Dr. Suhail and his son Fouad paid a visit to Ahmed's house. Ahmed graciously welcomed them into his home, fostering a strong friendship that had developed over time.

"How are things going?" Ahmed inquired.

Dr. Suhail expressed his concerns about the worsening situation under the gunmen's authority and sought advice from Ahmed on the matter. He explained that they had to make the difficult decision to leave due to the dangerous circumstances. He also shared the heartbreaking story of his son Fouad's postponed marriage to their neighbor's daughter Layla, whom he loved deeply.

Ahmed inquired about the rationale behind their decision to relocate, given their deep connections to the community.

Dr. Suhail explained that, despite their esteemed reputation and valuable contributions in the medical field, they faced challenges due to their refusal to comply with the strict regulations imposed by the armed individuals.

He elaborated on the reasons for their departure, including the hospital superintendent's affiliation with the gunmen group and the constant scrutiny of their appearance.

He recounted the tale of his wife, a gynecologist, and how the militants asked her to wear a niqab over her veil while working. Unfortunately, she received criticism for the thickness of her niqab from a woman who belonged to the militant group. In addition, the government has ceased paying salaries to individuals residing outside its controlled territory.

After a moment of reflection, Dr. Suhail expressed his gratitude to Ahmed for his friendship and support as they prepared to say their goodbyes.

Ahmed instructed him to keep this information hidden, avoid sharing it with anyone, regardless of how close they may be, and to offer money if necessary.

Dr. Suhail praised the man for his kindness and resilience, recognizing his commitment to his community. He showed his gratitude for his selfless actions by giving him $10,000 and the necessary medications to aid in his efforts. He said he knew that Ahmed would share the money with his neighbors and poor families in his region.

"I consider this a debt," Ahmed said upon receiving the money.

"Seize it immediately, and once we return safely, all problems will be straightforward," he asid.

Fouad visited Layla's house to bid her farewell, his heart aching with immense sorrow, feeling as though he was leaving a part of himself behind. He expressed his feelings, saying,

"Oh, my dearest love, as my body travels far, my heart, like a steadfast star, will remain with you. Despite the distance that separates us, our souls will intertwine forever in loving true."

He asked her to urge her family to expedite their migration so they could reunite promptly and he could be with his beloved.

Layla's emotional words and sorrowful expression were sincere and heartfelt.

"My heart goes with you too," she softly whispered, as if saying goodbye at a grave. They stood together, their emotions entwined in sorrow.

"From my eyes, the Tigris will flow, a river of sorrow, its currents aglow. Each tear that falls—a drop of pain—is a testament to a heart that's been slain."

Expressing her worry, she added, "I fear you will find someone new in your new home and forget about me completely."

With tears in his eyes, Fouad reassured her, telling her not to worry and to keep her heart cold because she is the only one he loves.

"Goodbye, Layla," he said with tears in his eyes before leaving and announcing, "Tonight we will depart."

Layla's heart is on the verge of breaking from grief as she bids farewell to the person she loves most. She had hoped to remain connected to him indefinitely, but an unexpected event has forced them apart. Despite her desire to join Fouad in migration, her father's stubbornness and refusal to leave their homeland have kept her from following her heart.

She remains behind, grappling with the pain of separation and the ache of longing for her beloved. Unable to find solace in sleep, Layla lies in bed, tears streaming down her face as she worries about Fouad and the dangers he may face on his journey. Seeking comfort, she often wanders into the garden, gazing at the moon as if searching for his presence in its glow.

In moments of desperation, Layla prays, "Oh my God, protect Fouad and his family, and watch over all travelers facing danger on their journeys."

4
They Miraculously Escape Death

Dr. Suhail returned to Ahmed's house three weeks later and rang the doorbell. Ahmed welcomed him, invited him to enter, and said, "I assumed you are currently in Baghdad."

"My dear, Ahmed, it is a long story!" he replied

"I hope it's a good story," Ahmed said.

All travel arrangements were in place when Dr. Suhail departed from Ahmed two weeks ago. On the second day, he left Mosul at daybreak with his family, passing through the districts of Tal Afar, Sinjar, and Baaj.

They stayed and slept at a friend's house in Baaj. The following day, they set out at 5:00 a.m. over muddy roads towards Al Qaim, a district in Al Ramadi Governorate near the Syrian border.

While on the road, they came across a gun patrol that ultimately compelled them to exit their car. They wanted to kill Fouad and his father; they separated them from Fouad's mother, blindfolded them, and took them to the foot of a deep valley, where they left them sitting. The patrol leader then ordered the group elements to prepare themselves for firing them. However, the deputy commander intervened, stating that they must inform their leadership before carrying out the execution.

The commander disagreed, arguing that the individuals were apostates for fleeing from areas under their control, and therefore, he took full responsibility for their deaths. A heated discussion ensued between the commander and his deputy, while the gunmen stood ready to fire upon receiving the commander's orders.

Throughout this tense situation, Fouad's mother was screaming and wailing at the top of her voice.

After the deputy made a call, a car arrived with a man who appeared to be in charge. He quickly intervened, reprimanding the patrol leader and questioning him. "How can you justify killing these people without a trial?"

The individual in charge decided to return Dr. Suhail to his wife and sent Fouad to prison in the Al-Baaj district pending the court's decision. He directed one of the armed individuals to accompany Dr. Suhail in his vehicle to ascertain his place of residence.

During the journey, Dr. Suhail inquired with the ISIS member about the potential sentence for Fouad. The response was grim: if there was no valid reason for their departure, both Fouad and Dr. Suhail could face execution. The ISIS member warned against mentioning a desire to return to work or leave due to harsh living conditions, as these were considered crimes. The only possible escape was a medical condition that required treatment unavailable in their current location.

Dr. Suhail visited his cousin Issa in Baaj and requested his help obtaining a medical report from Dr. Shatha in Mosul. The report was urgently required and should be about the suspicions of cancer in Fouad's mother's beast. Issa promptly travelled to Mosul, delivered a letter to Dr. Shatha from Dr. Khadija, and returned with the medical report within four days.

After receiving the report, Issa sought assistance from a friend who had connections with militants, and he requested that he visit Fouad in prison and persuade him to give false testimony in court. The testimony stated that they were traveling to Erbil for cancer detection and that the medical report was in the possession of his father.

Fouad remained in prison for two weeks, in a large hall with over fifty prisoners, unsure of when his turn for execution would come. Every day, an armed guard would come, and read out two or three names, announcing that they had been sentenced to death. Shortly after, he would take them away; Fouad and the other prisoners would hear gunshots, knowing that those individuals had been executed.

On the fifth day of his imprisonment, a gunman called out two names. Before he could speak, one of them protested, accusing the gunmen of being unjust and not true Muslims. The gunman responded by firing several shots, killing the protester. The blood spilled onto Fouad's clothes and face, and the gunman then took the second individual away.

Shortly after, a group of gunmen arrived to remove the body of the deceased. They provided cleaning supplies and instructed the prisoners to clean up the area.

On the tenth day of his imprisonment, an armed individual came and read out the name "Fouad." He answered "Yes" in a broken voice, barely swallowing his saliva, his heart racing as if it wanted to escape his chest. He began to think about Layla and what would happen to her when she learned of his execution. Then he started reciting the Shahada, as it is essential for a Muslim to recite the Shahada before death.

Furthermore, he remained silent as the person read out several other names. Suddenly, a person in the prison started groaning and screaming in pain, asking the armed individual to take him to the medical center or give him pain relief. Fouad and the others waited anxiously to hear what the armed individual would say about them, unsure if it would be the usual execution or release, which rarely happens. These few minutes felt like weeks, as the armed man did not want to speak a single word because he was preoccupied with the patient. This left everyone wondering about their fate.

Finally, the armed individual spoke and said, "Come with me," without explaining why; the situation increased their anxiety and left them feeling hopeless. They were then escorted into a car and told they were going to court.

The judge summoned Dr. Suhail to present the medical report and official permit during the trial. He explained that they had not obtained official permission for the trip due to the situation's urgency.

However, the judge imposed a $5,000 fine for failing to seek official permission and ordered him to return to Mosul to obtain the necessary permit before leaving again.

"That is why we decided to turn back, feeling disappointed," he said to Ahmed and his company.

Ahmed experienced relief and joy upon hearing of Dr. Suhail's safe return home and his son's release from prison. With great enthusiasm, he asked, "So, there are no other attempts, right?"

Dr. Suhail responded that he needed to leave by any means necessary. However, he admitted, "I made a grave error by driving my car. Smugglers can transport us in their vehicles, as they know where gun patrols are scarce and how to avoid detection. I plan to sell my car and depart."

"Why didn't you obtain an official exit permit if you had a report?" Ahmed inquired.

I am concerned that they will convene a medical committee to expose the inaccuracies in the report, potentially causing harm to the doctor who provided it.

Ahmed wished them a safe journey and requested that they inform him upon arrival, as he would await the news.

With great longing, as if he had been apart from Layla for a long time, Fouad returned to her, telling her the story of his imprisonment and impending death alongside his father. Then he asked, "How is my heart that I left with you?"

While gleefully crying, Layla answered, "Like my heart, you took it with you; if something bad happened to you, God forbid, I would not have enjoyed my life after you."

Then she asked, with tears streaming down her rosy cheeks.

"Didn't your father get the idea of immigration out of his mind?"

"No, emigration is the only option," He said, his eyes full of tears. "I hope you'll be able to join us as soon as possible. Your father is stubborn. I tried to convince him to join us, but he was not convinced."

"My father is not considering moving right now; he says I will not leave my country," she explained with sorrow.

Fouad stated that the days he spent apart from her were the most difficult days of his life. He shared with her his constant thoughts of her, especially during his captivity by gunmen.

During those days, she felt like she had lost something valuable. She only fell asleep after reaching complete exhaustion. He moved away to the outlet door and returned to Layla, giving her a deep stare and saying, "Bye, my love; we are leaving in one week, and my heart tells me we shall meet."

With tears streaming down her face, she kissed the palm of her hand and extended it toward him. With a wave of her hand, she whispered, her voice tinged with tears, "May God protect you, my darling."

5
USE OF MOBILE PHONES IS BANNED

Out of fear of being discovered, Ahmed would leave his phone in a room on the second floor, with a family member sitting nearby to inform him if someone called.

If caught using a phone, one faces severe penalties, including execution. Despite the prohibition of mobile credit, some individuals in government-controlled areas secretly transfer it to friends, family, and relatives.

"Father, someone is calling," Ahmed's son announced ten days after Fouad bid farewell to Layla.

"Hello, Dr. Suhail. How are you?" Ahmed greeted him as he answered the phone. "Where are you currently located? I trust that everything is going smoothly for you."

"I'm fine; I'm currently in Baghdad with my family. I may travel to Kirkuk in the coming days." He replied.

"Thank God for safety." Ahmed showed his joy and inquired, "How was your journey?"

Due to the extreme danger faced by those attempting to escape from gunmen control, the treacherous route has been dubbed the "Path of Perdition." The family members and friends remain concerned until one informs them that he or she has arrived in a safe location.

"The story is lengthy; these smugglers are adept at evading patrols by gunmen. Throughout our journey, we did not face any challenges," he responded.

When Layla was spending time with the phone, she stared at it while it was in quiet mode, and it was in her lap. Fouad might be able to reach her by phone. She received a call.

"My love, how is my heart with you?" Fouad asked,

Her eyes were welling up with tears.

"Why did you put off calling, Fouad?" she scolded. "You kept me worried; my heart was almost breaking."

"My love," Fouad answered. "I worry about you. I fear they will hear your voice while speaking on the phone, and something bad will happen to you." He paused, and tears welled up in his eyes. "As a result, I won't be contacting you much in the coming days. It would also be my downfall if something bad happened to you. I can handle the agony of distance, but I cannot bear losing you."

Two weeks after receiving a call from Fouad, Layla unlocked her mobile phone to discover a message waiting for her.

"In the vast expanse of my night sky, I endeavor to count the stars that lie.

With each beat and a rhythm so true, I feel your presence, as if on cue.

You, my love, are the guiding star, illuminating my world, near and far.

As the stars twinkle above, so bright, I think of you, my love, every night."

She sent the following words, replying.

"In the dark of night, where sleep eludes, your gentle shadow, my solace, intrudes.

Amidst the chaos that engulfs my thoughts, I find comfort in your presence, like soothing breaths.

Oh, how your soft silhouette brings me peace—a balm for my weary soul's release.

Like a gentle breeze on a summer's day, your presence brings solace, come what may."

She copied these words into a notebook and deleted messages and contacts from the phone's memory. She went to her room and left the phone on the sofa in the guest's room, as her mind was preoccupied.

They heard a knock on the door a little while later. When her father, Othman, opened it, he discovered many gunmen.

"Salam alaikum," the leader greeted Othman. "We're looking for firearms. Bring a gun, if you have one. If not, we do a comprehensive search of the home."

"I don't have any weapons," Othman retorted. "Please enter and search."

The leader told his group, "Two of you enter with me," and ordered the others to wait in front of the door. They quickly made their way into the house and the guest's room.

"What is this cellphone? Who were you speaking with?" He asked in a harsh tone.

"We didn't talk to anyone, and the phone is devoid of credit." Othman replied,

"Perhaps somebody called you? The group leader said:

Othman denied that "neither we nor anyone else called anyone."

"So why is the phone on the sofa here? Did you not hear that we forbade cell phones?

Layla overheard the conversation, put on her niqab, and hurried over, saying,

"I was playing games on my cellphone, so I left it here. Even though the phone has no password, you can check the call history to see if there have been any calls or messages."

The leader checked the call and message logs, but he could not find anything. They requested that Othman accompany them to the police station, but he was hesitant to go, leading them to attempt to arrest him. Layla and her mother intervened to stop Othman's arrest, but one of the armed individuals kicked Layla's mother, causing her to fall to the ground. Layla and her mother spent days waiting anxiously for Othman's return, but he never came back, leaving them in tears day and night.

Layla and her mother were still perplexed and unsure of what to do. Disasters follow her, adding to her already heavy load and deepening her sorrow.

"My God," Layla cried out. "My father and my fiancé were the two men I used to count on when things were bad. Whom do I cling to now that neither of them exists? My God, you are my support; please provide me comfort."

She approached her mother and expressed her intention to seek assistance from Sheikh Ahmed. She had hoped that Sheikh Ahmed could reach out to Fouad on her behalf and warn him not to call her at her current number, which ISIS had taken. She expressed concern that if any calls were to reach their current number, it may jeopardize her father's safety and potentially lead to harm.

The mother inquired whether she was aware of his residential address. Layla reacted by stating that, due to his fame, it is highly likely that a significant number of cab drivers are acquainted with his residential address.

Layla, accompanied by her younger sibling Omer, left their home wearing her niqab. She confidently hailed a taxi and instructed the driver to take them to Sheikh Ahmed's residence. The driver, familiar with Ahmed's address, skillfully navigated them to their destination.

Upon arrival, Layla rang the doorbell. Ahmed emerged and was surprised to see a young girl and boy at his doorstep. Without hesitation, he called his wife and warmly welcomed Layla inside. Grateful for the hospitality, Layla introduced herself as the daughter of Othman. She expressed her thanks and explained that she had a request to make before returning home.

Ahmed listened attentively and assured Layla that he was willing to help with any needs or requests she may have.

She asked him to contact Fouad and tell him that armed men had arrested her father and confiscated her phone. Therefore, she requested that he refrain from contacting them at that number to avoid endangering her father's life.

Ahmed graciously invited her inside to join his wife for a seat, and while she savored her coffee, he promised to contact Fouad once she provided him with the phone number.

Five minutes had elapsed since Layla and her brother arrived when Ahmed emerged and declared, "I relayed the information to him over the phone; therefore, he will not contact you at that number." Pausing briefly, he added, "Please inform me of your father's whereabouts; I will visit him tomorrow."

She informed Ahmed of the location of her father's captivity, while tears ran down her cheeks in an agitated voice.

Ahmed approached the prison official on the second day and inquired, "Why have you imprisoned this unfortunate man?"

"We discovered a mobile phone in his residence, resting on the sofa," the prison official responded.

Ahmed, visibly upset, retorted, "Why does that matter? It is not a weapon of mass destruction."

The prison officer, with a stern tone, declared, "Are they not aware that mobile phones are strictly prohibited?"

"His daughter was simply playing a game on it." Ahmed countered Please consider releasing him; he is the sole provider for his family. There is no one else to take care of them in his absence."

"We will give it one week; if calls will not come to the phone, we will set him free." The official stated it firmly.

Ten days had gone by, and Othman had still not returned. Layla and her mother were unable to stop their tears from flowing.

Determined to find answers, Layla's mother declared, "I will go to them." With her young son, Omar, by her side, she made her way to the prison official to inquire about Othman's delayed release.

After questioning the prison official, Layla's mother demanded an explanation as to the reason for Othman's delayed release, as previously stated. The official explained that he had not yet stood trial.

In disbelief, Layla's mother retorted, "Has he committed a crime that warrants such a delay in justice?" The prison official comforted her by confirming that Othman would face the judiciary the following day to decide his future. With a heavy heart, Layla's mother had no option but to wait for two more days to see how events would unfold.

6
Supplies are Running out, and Prices are Skyrocketing

The deterioration in quality of life became apparent as individuals encountered growing obstacles in their daily lives. Harassment resulted in a decrease in personal freedoms, such as restrictions on clothing options, facial hair length, and other aspects of their appearance.

With each passing day, things got worse, as the government stopped paying salaries for staff that remained in the area under gunmen's control a few months after they gained control, as well as gasoline, supplies, and electricity. Prices were rising, individuals were running out of money, and earning opportunities were dwindling or nonexistent for most people, particularly food and medication.

To survive, some teenagers and even young toddlers have begun to enlist as gunmen or work for them in various jobs.

Experts have determined that the purposeful hold-up in the liberation of armed group-controlled territory is a calculated move to facilitate the influx of thousands of militants into Mosul, which will have an impact on the huge destruction of the city and its inhabitants. This delay has also served to strengthen the armed groups' misleading rhetoric, in which they claim to be liberating the region from Western and Iranian domination. As a result, thousands more people from various regions of Iraq and beyond flooded the conflict zone.

Several governmental and international media outlets amplified this propaganda. However, those who were not under the gunmen's control were unaware of the extreme suffering the people had to endure.

Many individuals joined the gunmen out of desperation rather than choice, whether by choice or coercion, and endured great difficulties alongside their loved ones in the aftermath. Following the liberation, they faced challenges from the government, leading to the incarceration of a substantial number of these individuals, as well as numerous innocent civilians uninvolved with the gunmen. Sadly, many of them remain imprisoned to this day.

Additionally, their families were unable to return home until they publicly disowned their sons in governmental tribunals. As a result, many migrated permanently away from the country.

****

Fouad grew anxious about Layla's and her family's safety. He came to the realization that his mother-in-law's phone was out of reach of the telecommunications network after repeatedly attempting to contact her through calls and messages, yet receiving no response. Separation from the person with whom he had intended to spend the remainder of his life is dreadful, especially if he was unaware of her whereabouts during his absence. A blazing fire was piercing his heart. He occasionally has a great desire to visit Layla.

"My father," Fouad said hesitantly, "I want to visit Layla; I'm feeling very anxious."

"Have you considered your studies?" his father inquired. "And if you venture into the gunmen's territory, can you guarantee your safety once more?" After a moment of contemplation, he continued, "I strongly advise against going."

"Well, Father, how can I stay informed about Layla and her family?" Fouad inquired.

"Contact Sheikh Ahmed; he is known for his generosity, bravery, and willingness to help. I am sure to provide you with the information you seek," his father suggested.

"Okay, Dad, I will reach out to him," Fouad responded.

Fouad's uneasiness increased when he failed to reach his mother-in-law's mobile phone and when he had not heard from Layla or her family. This feeling grew stronger after learning of his father-in-law's incarceration.

Following his initial hesitation to reach Sheikh Ahmed, as his dad recommended owing to his shyness, he ultimately collected the courage to call him.

Ahmed's son called his father, saying, "Dad, the phone is ringing; it's merely number-calling."

"Hello, who am I speaking to?" Ahmed answered.

"I'm Fouad. I'll try not to keep you on the line too long." He expressed his concern for Layla and her family, inquiring about his father-in-law's situation in jail. Fouad stated that he had attempted to contact them via his mother-in-law's phone, but it was out of range of the telecom network. His mind was weary from constant thoughts, and his heart felt like it was on the verge of bursting from lack of sleep.

Ahmed, speaking with a touch of compassion, asked him, "Please provide me with their address, and I will personally go check on them. I will give you an update if you call me tomorrow afternoon."

When Ahmed finally visited Layla's father, he received the delightful news that Othman was free. Additionally, he learned that the provider had deactivated the SIM card on Layla's mother's phone due to prolonged inactivity.

Tears welled in Layla's eyes as she turned to Ahmed and asked, "Uncle Ahmed, how can I send a letter to Fouad?"

With compassion in his voice, Ahmed replied, "Don't worry, it's simple. Just write it, and I'll ensure it reaches him."

The following day, Fouad contacted Ahmed to inquire about Layla and her family. Without hesitation, Ahmed provided him with the latest information.

7
They Got Stuck in the Desert

Dr. Essam is a university lecturer known for his strict, self-confident, and stubborn nature, as well as his tall and graceful stature, raspy voice, and stylish attire. He recently visited Sheikh Ahmed with a significant decision on his mind.

"I am considering emigrating to Baghdad or Kirkuk, and I came to seek your advice and bid farewell," Dr. Essam informed Sheikh Ahmed.

Ahmed, taken aback by the boldness of Essam's plan, expressed his concerns. "Do you not realize the difficulty and danger of attempting to escape at this time? If they catch anyone trying to flee their controlled areas, he faces the risk of killing or arrest," Ahmed cautioned.

Undeterred, Dr. Essam explained his reasoning. "Ahmed, I feel compelled to enroll in an alternative university in Kirkuk out of fear that I may lose my current position," he revealed.

In a gesture of support, Ahmed offered financial assistance to Essam, who politely declined, demonstrating that he had sufficient funds. Essam then presented Ahmed with supplies he had gathered, including sacks of flour and bulgur, cooking oil, sugar, and canned goods from his own reserves.

"Please take these items with you; they will be necessary," Dr. Essam instructed.

"I insist on covering the cost, as it is quite a lot," Ahmed offered.

Dr. Essam firmly declined any financial compensation, stating, "Consider it a gift."

"May Allah bless you and your belongings," Ahmed prayed, offering advice. "Please ensure the road is safe."

"Absolutely," Dr. Essam replied. "I must verify the safety of the road before embarking on the journey."

Ahmed expressed his heartfelt wish for Dr. Essam and his family to reach their destination safely.

A few days after this conversation, Dr. Essam traveled to the Al-Hatra district, stayed overnight with his friend Samir, and confided in him that he was planning to sneak into Baghdad.

Samir paid a visit to one of his relatives who participated in illegal smuggling. During their meeting, he subtly asked about potential escape routes.

He returned home late at night and told Essam about it.

"There are two methods of travel," Samir elaborated. "The smuggling route passes through urban areas, where armed patrols regularly patrol the area. There is a significant risk of encountering these patrols while traveling on this route, which could result in arrest. Travelers must conceal themselves in the valleys during the day and drive without lights at night until they reach Tharthar Lake. From there, they can proceed to the Heet district or Ramadi City, the central hub of the Al-Anber governorate. Next, they would travel to the Ain al-Tamr district, which falls under the jurisdiction of Karbala and is governed by the government. Finally, the journey would continue from Karbala to Baghdad."

And he told him that after leaving the gunmen-controlled territory, he would have to pass through numerous checkpoints. Some of these road checkpoints are soft, while others are harsh, especially when it comes to young people.

He mentioned that the second route is a desert road on which you must drive for more than five hours without stopping. The route traverses a desolate desert landscape, where encounters with other individuals are rare. If the car breaks down, it could take weeks before you see an individual there.

After receiving valuable knowledge from Samir, Dr. Essam brought it back with him upon his return. Following a period of rest, Essam gathered his family to discuss the two distinct routes available to them, along with the potential risks associated with each.

Israa, Essam's wife, is a delicate woman of petite stature. She expressed a preference for taking the smuggler road, but Essam decided to venture through the desert instead. Accompanying him on this journey were his two children: Arqam, his eldest son, a 17-year-old with a devout nature, a robust build, and a proclivity for obesity; and Simak, his youngest son, who shared his curiosity about the desert.

Dr. Essam had $50,000 in his possession. He decided to hide $35,000 in a secret compartment in his car, keeping $5,000 and five million Iraqi dinars for road expenses. He discreetly handed his wife $10,000 and instructed her to keep it hidden. This precaution was taken because women typically receive less thorough searches at checkpoints. Dr. Essam loaded the car trunk with food, water, and canned goods, preparing for their journey. At 8:00 a.m., they departed for the sub-district of Tal Abta, where they planned to seek refuge with a relative named Abdul-Rahman.

Upon arrival, Dr. Essam informed Abdul Rahman of his intention to flee, who welcomed him with open arms. Abdul-Rahman's wife prepared enough food for the family to last several days, while Abdul-Rahman himself brought along 10 two-liter bottles of soft drinks.

As night fell, Samir contacted Dr. Essam, urging him to call upon reaching a city to confirm his safety. The group set out on their journey, filled with hope and determination.

Essam embarked on a journey with his family at 4:00 a.m., driving slowly and without lights. After two hours, the darkness lifted, and the road became visible. It was a desolate and isolated road, devoid of any signs of life.

"Essam, I feel like we're in the midst of a limitless sea; the landscape seems eerie, barren, and unsettling." I can feel my chest tightening." Israa remarked,

"There is little time left to cross this desert," Essam chuckled. "I want you to appreciate the beauty of the desert. You have never seen anything like it. Imagine the mirage before you, resembling a shimmering lake. Have you ever beheld such a captivating illusion?"

"It's a breathtaking view, Mom," Arqam exclaimed with a wide grin.

The smooth, bump-free desert road tempted Essam to accelerate. Within minutes, he fell asleep, only to awaken to discover the car drifting off the road and becoming stuck in the sand. The car continued to sink deeper into the mud despite his attempts to free it by pressing the gas pedal.

The family attempted to push the car, but to no avail.

"Didn't I warn you, Essam, about the risks of this desolate road?" Israa yelled. "What are we going to do? We are currently stuck in this place until our resources run out, and we may not survive."

"Stay calm, Israa," Essam reassured her. "Let's brainstorm and find a way out of this predicament."

Arqam, trying to lighten the mood, said, "Mom, let's pretend we are on a desert camping trip."

"Arqam, this is no time for jokes," Israa snapped.

Essam, with a grin on his face, said, "Don't worry, my dear wife. Every problem has a solution."

Israa, growing more frustrated, demanded, "What solution, Essam?"

"I will find a solution for us," Essam promised confidently as he gazed at Israa with a reassuring smile. He swiftly pulled out his cell phone and dialed Samir's number, but his expression quickly changed to one of frustration. Turning away from Israa, he muttered, "I am unable to access the telecommunications network for some reason."

Israa's frustration boiled over, and she exclaimed, "This is just another obstacle that seems to leave us no choice but to perish."

"Calm down, dear mother," Arqam interjected, trying to soothe her. "Arguing won't help us when facing death. If it is our time to go, let us accept it. And if God wants us to survive, He will provide a way, even if it is not in our minds.

"Your mother has done an excellent job raising strong men." Essam praised.

"Come with me, Simak," Arqam called to his brother. "We will gather some desert bushes."

Together, they ventured out and collected around 25 bushes. Arqam skillfully used a knife to trim the branches and then proceeded to connect the trunks using wires from the car. He constructed two pillars, each about two and a half meters tall. With the car serving as one side of the shelter, Arqam created an improvised structure by placing the two pillars on the other side and covering them with a blanket to shield them from the scorching sun.

They sat silently for an extended period; no one wanted to speak to prevent Israa from unleashing a flood of words, especially since her eyes were filled with tears.

The desert is a place of strange paradoxes: the scorching sun beats down, the heat feels unbearable, and the wind carries sand like a fiery storm. The landscape changes with the wind, making it seem as if the sand is flowing like water.

During the night, the desert is eerie and quiet, devoid of any signs of life. There are no animals, birds, or vegetation, apart from lonely bushes scattered across the vast expanse.

The mirage of a distant lake taunts you, always moving further away as you approach. The vast emptiness of the desert can make your chest feel tight and uneasy, despite the seemingly endless space.

"We must use water and food sparingly," Essam said, breaking the silence, "so that we can stay alive as long as possible; maybe someone will come by here," he added after a few seconds of silence. "We pray our prayers with tayammum, using no water. When the food and water run out, we drink soft drinks, as they contain sugar, and thus compensate for the food and water."

Israa began to prepare lunch, muttering, "You didn't hear me, even though I knew it was dangerous. But men are risk-takers and adventurous by nature; what kind of people are they whose souls are so cheap that they are willing to risk their lives and laugh in the face of death?"

After eating and praying to ward off the fear of snakes and scorpions, they decided to sleep in the car. Essam occasionally climbs onto the top of the car, hopping to spot someone, but to no avail.

"What are you looking for?" asked Israa. "Who comes from this lonely road except the crazy ones?"

Essam and the children laughed heartily for an extended period, causing Arqam to join in with his uncontrollable laughter.

"I've never seen anyone like you, waiting to die and laughing with your mouths full," Israa shouted angrily.

"Don't worry, my beloved wife; I have faith that Samir will come looking for us sooner or later," Essam said.

Over the course of three days, they alternated between exploring during the day, seeking shelter under the umbrella, and retreating to the car at night. Arqam's jokes never failed to elicit laughter from Essam and Simak, while Israa found their amusement grating and incendiary, her face eternally twisted in a grimace and frown.

"I want to make you laugh." Arqam said to his mother,

"Arqam, you are a good boy, but please do not disturb me." She replied, "This is not the appropriate time for laughter."

Arqam persisted, "Allow me to share a true story that recently occurred to me."

He began to recall a memorable incident from his eighth-grade year when they assigned him to deliver a speech on Teacher's Day. As he reminisced, a smile played on his lips. "I stood before a packed auditorium, filled with teachers and students eagerly awaiting my words.

"I stood up, feeling disoriented as my vision blurred. As I made my way up the stairs to the podium, I stumbled and fell, causing laughter to fill the hall and adding to my confusion. Two of my friends quickly came to my aid, lifting me up. They placed a small table under the pupils' feet so that they could stand at the podium and have their heads appear over it.

Despite my height, I climbed onto the table and began to speak. Looking out at the audience, all I could see were blurry figures resembling ghosts. My voice cracked, sweat dripped down my body, and my legs trembled uncontrollably. I lost my balance and fell off the table. Two of my friends lifted me up and placed me back in front of the podium. Determined not to fall again, I gripped the podium tightly as the laughter in the room grew louder. I expressed my gratitude to everyone for their attentive listening before concluding my reading; the audience responded with a round of applause and an eruption of laughter."

They erupted in laughter, and Israa couldn't contain her giggle as she joined in. She laughed until she was on her back. Essam expressed gratitude to Arqam for making Israa laugh so much.

On the fourth day, Essam was outside the car in the afternoon and noticed two animals approaching. The fact that these animals resembled dogs indicated that a human might have been nearby.

The youngest and only female child of three years in the family, Aisha, excitedly exclaimed, "Daddy means salvation has come."

"Be happy, my little sister," Arqam reassured her. "Increase your prayers, remember God more, and may peace be upon the Messenger of God; help will come."

Essam, upon seeing the two creatures clearly, quickly identified them: "They are wolves, not dogs."

Aisha's body began to tremble in fear. "Papa, I'm scared. Wolves are known to be man-eaters."

"We are safe in the car, sister," Simak said, trying to calm her down.

In reality, Simak was terrified, but he wanted to appear brave.

Israa broke down once again at the sight of the wolves: "I don't mind starving to death, but I can't bear the thought of wolves eating us. How will we go to the bathroom? How will we eat?"

"Let's sleep on it tonight, and remember, as the saying goes, tomorrow is another day," Arqam suggested.

At times, the wolves would climb on top of the car and loom directly above the cabin. Israa and Aisha were filled with fear, but eventually exhaustion overtook them, and they fell asleep.

When Essam woke up early for his morning prayers, he found the two wolves sprawled out with their paws near the car. Wanting to avoid startling anyone, he gently woke the family before quickly honking the car horn and keeping his finger on it. The wolves backed away and moved to a safe distance from the car. None of the family members were willing to exit the car because they were afraid of finding themselves unexpectedly surrounded by the pair of wolves.

"It's nearly noon, and we are in desperate need of relieving ourselves," Arqam stated. "I have a plan."

"Please tell us," Essam inquired. "What do you propose?"

Arqam explained, "I will retrieve three steel pots and three dishes from the trunk. Three of us—you, me, and Simak—will confront the wolves by banging on the pots with the dishes to create enough noise to scare them away."

Israa pleaded with them to reconsider. "I'm worried for your safety, please."

"You, Arqam, are a true hero," Essam commended. "That's a brilliant idea; we must take action."

"I will count to three, and then we will attack together," Arqam instructed.

They all rushed at the wolves, knocking on the pots and dishes simultaneously.

The animals fled, and they pursued them for a significant distance.

After performing the tayammum and the traveling prayers, they sat around their meal.

Following the Maghrib and Eisha prayers, they settled down to rest in the car. Just before midnight, they spotted the wolves once more.

"There must be water nearby; otherwise, the wolves would have perished from thirst," Essam remarked.

The following morning, Essam woke up at dawn to pray and realized that the wolves were not present. He promptly woke up the rest of the family to join him for morning prayer. After evacuating themselves, performing dry ablution, and completing their prayers, they gathered in the car. Israa kindly served breakfast, which they enjoyed before heading back to the safety of the car. They remained cautious, as they were still wary of the wolves potentially returning without warning.

In the afternoon, the group spotted the wolves returning once again. Aisha and Simak expressed their hunger, prompting Israa to feel apprehensive about leaving the safety of the car to prepare lunch.

Arqam confidently declared, "I will scare them off with the pot, just like last time." Despite his father's warning that he couldn't do it alone, Arqam exited the car, leaving the door open, and charged towards one of the wolves while banging the pot loudly. The wolf fled, but the other wolf, from a distance, lunged at Arqam. He sprinted back to the car, managing to slip inside and shut the door just in time. However, the wolf managed to grab hold of him, ripping his shirt sleeve and scratching his right hand from the upper arm down to the forearm. Arqam forcefully closed the door, trapping the wolf's arm inside, causing it to yelp and thrash about.

Essam swiftly grabbed a knife and began striking the wolf's foot in an attempt to injure it, hoping it would retreat and not return. Arqam then opened the car door a little, causing the wolf to release its grip and flee, howling in pain. The two wolves vanished and did not return again for three days.

Essam descended from the car, retrieved the first aid kit, sterilized Arqam's wounded hand, and bandaged it up.

After the incident, they stayed in the car for two days, only venturing out to eat, pray, and evacuate before quickly returning due to fear of the wolves. Arqam's hand began to swell and hurt, prompting Essam to comment, "It seems like the wound has become infected." As night fell, the two wolves once again approached them.

Israa, overwhelmed with emotion, cried out, "Why are we stuck in this desolate place? In this wilderness, our son's hand is deteriorating."

Arqam attempted to reassure his mother, saying, "Please remain calm, mother. We cannot escape what fate has in store for us. Have faith; every distress must have relief."

Israa continued to cry, especially when she looked at Arqam's injured hand.

****

Samir was growing increasingly concerned as about one week had gone by without a call from Essam. This lack of communication indicated they were likely in an area without a telecommunications network. Since the journey along this route usually only takes a day under normal circumstances, Samir began to worry that they might have become lost.

He sought out his cousin, a skilled smuggler, and shared his story, saying, "I will give you whatever you desire; come with me; we must track them down. I cannot rest with worry; he is a cherished friend."

"Whoever is important to you is important to me," his relative stated. "I will accompany you without expecting anything in return. It is a matter of humanity to assist others, as those who help will get rewards in paradise. Please gather all necessary supplies by 5:00 a.m. We will then begin our search for their location."

At 5:00 a.m., Samir and the smuggler set off. Samir packed enough food and water for several days. By the time Essam awoke at nearly 7 o'clock, the wolves were nowhere in sight. He opened the door, climbed onto the roof, and spotted an approaching vehicle. With excitement, he shouted, "Allah Akbar" (God is great).

The entire family woke up. "What is happening?" Israa inquired. Essam joyfully exclaimed, "A car is approaching; help has arrived!"

"Praise be to God!" echoed throughout the group. As Essam stepped out of the car, he warmly welcomed them and embraced Samir, tears streaming down their faces.

"I had a strong feeling that you would come," Essam told Samir. He then embraced the smuggler, expressing gratitude for their timely arrival.

The smuggler, thankful for everyone's safety, began clearing the sand from behind Essam's car with a shovel. They worked together, taking turns, until they reached the road. Using a sturdy rope from his vehicle, the smuggler attached it to Essam's car and pulled it backward. Samir and the family pushed from the front, successfully freeing the car onto the road.

With a sense of relief and gratitude, the family thanked God for their safety.

Samir extended an invitation for them to accompany him back to his home, emphasizing that he would not allow them to continue on the treacherous desert road. Essam, aware of the urgency due to Arqam's need for immediate treatment, assured them that the designated place was only a few hours away.

Israa expressed her reluctance to revisit the dangerous path, recalling their previous escape from the wolves. Aisha, fearing the wolves, pleaded with her father to turn back.

Samir, recognizing the danger of the desert route, advised Essam to abandon the idea and offered that his relative would take them out of the ISIS-controlled area.

Essam, convinced by the group's consensus, agreed to return.

Samir then suggested they rest and recuperate at his house before embarking on the journey with his relatives to escape the ISIS-controlled areas.

"I don't believe so," Israa stated. "While I appreciate your invitation and respect your perspective, I believe it would be most beneficial for us to head back to Mosul and enjoy a week-long vacation. We could both benefit from some relaxation. My mind is constantly wandering, and we also need to tend to Arqam's hand."

"We will head back to Mosul and return to visit you in a week, dear Samir," Essam assured him.

"Whenever you require our assistance, we will be there for you," Samir responded.

Essam and his family had returned to Mosul. Upon their arrival, they unloaded the car and began packing up their belongings.

They immediately brought Arqam to the doctor, who sterilized his wound, prescribed antibiotics, and recommended daily check-ups for wound care. After returning from the doctor, Arqam confidently declared, "I am going to take a two-hour nap after prayer; no one ever bothers to wake me up."

After a refreshing shower, Essam decided to pay a visit to Sheikh Ahmed. He felt compelled to see him, as he had claimed to have spent a significant amount of time sleeping in the desert.

Ahmed was deep in conversation with Yusuf, a visitor from Shirqat, and Sheikh Rifaat, a respected Muslim religious leader, when the ringing of the bell abruptly interrupted their discussion. Ahmed warmly welcomed Dr. Essam at the door and leaned in to whisper, "Have you not traveled?"

Essam responded with a smile, stating that the silver screen will forever capture our amazing tale. He recounted the challenging experiences they had endured, highlighting the obstacles and triumphs that shaped their journey.

"Thank God you are safe," Ahmed chuckled. "It would take a skilled scriptwriter to turn this into a movie. What's next? Have you let go of the idea of leaving, or are you still set on it?"

"I am determined to leave," Essam replied. "I would rather enter the lion's den than stay here any longer."

"Your next escape will be the sequel," Ahmed added, grinning.

"Make me the hero of the series," Yusuf joked.

8
Essam's Family Embarks on another Endeavor

It took three weeks to properly treat Arqam's wound, during which Essam informed his family to prepare for another escape. He announced that they would be leaving the following day.

"I'm freaking out," Israa blurted.

"Don't worry, everything is in God's hands," Dr. Essam reassured her. "Remember how we miraculously made it out of the desert last time? We'll be fine."

Sheikh Ahmed visited Dr. Essam, who welcomed him warmly. "Good news, come on in," he said.

"Thanks, but I have company waiting for me at home," Ahmed replied. "Please relay this message to Fouad, the son of Dr. Suhail; call him once you arrive in Kirkuk. He is dealing with some love troubles."

They headed to Samir in the Al-Hatra district.

"Dear Samir, please inform your smuggling friend that I urgently need to leave this region."

"Why the rush? Take a breather for a couple of days," Samir suggested.

"The longer I wait, the worse it gets," Essam explained.

Samir tried to locate the smuggler, but found him sleeping. "When your dad wakes up, send him my way tonight," he told his son.

Late that night, the smuggler finally arrived at Samir's place. Essam struck a deal with him to safely navigate them out of ISIS territory, agreeing to pay whatever was necessary.

"So, we're taking the scenic road through the desert, huh?" the smuggler joked.

Israa was not amused. "There's no way I'm going through that path, and neither are you."

When it became clear the smuggler was joking, everyone shared a laugh, including Israa, who couldn't contain her amusement.

The smuggler graciously informed Essam that he would be transporting Abu Sarhan's family in his minibus that night, directing him to follow in his own vehicle. He specified that they would be departing just two hours past midnight, ensuring that everyone was prepared and ready to go. In a gesture of true kindness, Samir offered Essam financial assistance, declaring him a brother. Essam politely declined, stating that he had more than enough money to cover the expenses.

The group set off on their journey at the early hour of 2 a.m., driving without lights. Finally, after three hours of driving, they arrived in a deep valley and moved off the path to remain hidden. The plan was to stay put until after dark, then quietly depart without any lights.

As they settled in, everyone performed ablution and prayer. Aisha, the youngest member of the group, innocently asked her father about the consequences of skipping a single prayer for fear the patrols would expose them. Her brother, Arqam, reassured her that a true Muslim never neglects their prayers. Aisha, providing some comic relief, requested water to wash her hands before praying, causing laughter among the group.

Tension mounted as the smuggler warned them to stay silent to avoid attracting attention from ISIS patrols in the area. Two hours after sunset, the convoy set off under the cloak of darkness, driving without lights as the skilled driver effortlessly guided them along the familiar route.

Suddenly, a light appeared behind them, rapidly approaching. The smuggler pressed the gas pedal, racing against time to reach the valley before the light caught up. They veered off the road and sought refuge in the valley, where they stayed hidden in their vehicles.

The approaching light revealed an armed patrol as they advanced through the valley towards the convoy's intended destination. The smuggler advised the group to wait for the patrol to return before attempting to leave, as encountering them on the road would likely lead to capture.

After an hour, the patrol turned back in the direction they had come from. The smuggler urged the convoy to make haste and depart before another patrol arrived. They quickly left the valley, reaching the Heet district before continuing on to Ramadi, the capital of the al-Anbar governorate. After resting and enjoying a hearty breakfast, they set off for Ain al-Tamr district, which belongs to Karbala governorate in the south of Iraq.

"The government's military and popular mobilization forces are in charge of Ain al-Tamr," the smuggler explained. When Dr. Essam asked if there were any contacts willing to help them there, the smuggler replied, "There are no allies in that area. You must look out for yourselves."

It was eight o'clock in the morning when they arrived at Ain al-Tamr. "Abu Sarhan," the smuggler said, "after passing the checkpoint, a car would be waiting for you. Here is the driver's contact information. Please reach out to him to arrange a meeting location.

"Dr. Essam, try to follow Abu Sarhan," the smuggler said.

As they prepared to part ways, the smuggler wished everyone safety and security. Dr. Essam, accompanied by his family, made their way to the Ain al-Tamr checkpoint. They easily passed through the initial security check after Dr. Essam mentioned his intention to join Mosul University in Kirkuk and confirmed his status as a professor at the university. The next checkpoint, which was more challenging, was only a three-minute drive away.

The control officer asked, "Where are you from and where are you headed?"

"We're leaving Mosul and going to Baghdad," Essam answered.

"You are from the city of terrorists!" The officer declared,

"Mosul inhabitants are not affiliated with any terrorist groups." With great vehemence, Dr. Essam shot back.

"What prevented you from opposing them?" inquired the officer.

"What? Could we use knives to fight them?" Essam paused and then inquired, "Why did the army confiscate all our firearms and search every home for weapons several times, leaving us defenseless?" He then pointed accusingly at the officer and exclaimed, "You should direct this question to all armed forces: why did they abandon their weapons and flee?"

"It seems that your conversation is a bit too loud," the control officer remarked.

"Why are you so upset when I am simply speaking the truth about what has happened?" Essam shot back, clearly furious.

Israa approached and explained, "The exhaustion is obvious to my husband. We found ourselves stranded in the vast desert, facing imminent death. He has been driving non-stop for three days with very little sleep." He is also a professor at the university. Please, can you allow us to pass?"

As they approached the checkpoint, the officer asked for identification from each person. Dr. Essam politely handed over the family's ID cards. The officer then requested that they wait while he called a soldier to input their names into a computer for verification.

An hour later, the soldier returned with everyone's ID cards except for Arqam's. "Sir, Arqam's name matches that of a wanted individual," the soldier explained.

"Where is Arqam?" The officer demanded, "Bring him here immediately."

"Please understand me; I am a university professor, and this is my son, who is a student; it is highly unlikely that he has any connection to ISIS," Dr. Essam pleaded.

"The names are identical. We must detain him for further investigation. If he is innocent, we will release him," the officer stated firmly.

"If you dare to detain him, he will inevitably find himself behind bars, surrounded by a sea of other unfortunate souls," Dr. Essam remarked with a touch of sarcasm. "Oh, my dear, he's just a child; how could you possibly justify taking him away?"

The officer retorted, "It seems you lack faith in our judicial system."

Dr. Essam raised his eyebrows, exclaiming loudly, "Anyone you decide to detain will languish in captivity for months on end before even catching a glimpse of the ruler."

"Do you actually believe we're criminals?" The commanding officer scoffed at Essam. "Please, try to stay within the confines of reality and don't cross your limit."

"My dear," Essam said. "Thousands of individuals in Iraq share the same full name, yet each person possesses unique characteristics and distinctions," Essam remarked. "You can determine if a name is correct by analyzing the differences in the person's age, marital status, mother's name, clan, and sibling names. My dear, you spoke of a suspicion, which implies that it is merely a suspicion. Do you arrest people on suspicion alone?"

"This is the protocol," the officer replied with a hint of sarcasm.

"Sir, go ahead and kill us all here; just make sure to leave my son alone," Israa said defiantly. "I swear, we're not going anywhere until you release him."

"Mom," Arqam interjected calmly, "please leave and do not worry. It is clear to me that I have done nothing to warrant imprisonment. When they eventually release me, I will find my way back to you."

"Oh, my dear son, do you honestly believe that anyone who has spent years rotting away in prison has anything of value to go to jail for? Look at this fine officer here; he's a shining example of justice and fairness." "I'm sure many of those poor souls, like you, had suspicion," he added, fixing his gaze on the officer."

"Excuse me," Israa firmly stated. "I already informed you that my husband is exhausted. Please allow us to pass." She continued saying, following a short moment of silence, that "he is in a state of devastation due to the unjust removal of our son, which is the reason for his extreme distress. Please understand his frustration." Israa pointed at the officer, with her index finger emphasizing her words. "Imagine if your child was innocent and ripped away from you. How would you feel?"

The officer, displaying arrogance and authority, replied, "You may proceed. We will conduct a thorough investigation into your son's case and release him promptly if we find him innocent. That is all I have to say."

Dr. Essam, visibly agitated, attempted to speak out, but Israa intervened, urging him to remain calm. "You're exhausted from driving. Take a moment to relax," she advised, concerned that any outburst could lead to his arrest.

"Sir," Israa declared firmly, "we are determined to stay until our son returns to us safely, no matter how long it may take—be it days, months, or even a year."

The officer nonchalantly responded, "Feel free to stay. Where do you plan on setting up camp?"

Israa, with a touch of sarcasm, retorted, "Perhaps we'll pitch a tent right here! We are not going anywhere. Whether you choose to detain us, harm us, or release our son, we are prepared for any outcome."

Unfazed, the officer maintained his icy demeanor. "You are welcome to stay as long as you wish, but do not expect a swift resolution. You may be here for a year."

Essam exclaimed, "This situation is truly unbelievable; as I had foreseen, if you take our son, he would end up and rot in prison. And now, to our surprise, you are proposing that we remain here for a year."

A sense of sadness and despair enveloped the family, leaving them feeling lost and uncertain about their next steps. In their desperation, they turned to a higher power for guidance. They spent several nights sleeping in their car and aimlessly wandering during the day, feeling trapped in this cycle for what seemed like an eternity.

Murtadha, a compassionate soldier, took pity on their plight and made it his mission to provide them with food and drink twice a day, despite their obvious lack of appetite. However, a glimmer of hope emerged on the horizon as a light appeared, hinting that there might finally be a way out of this seemingly endless ordeal.

A few days later, the entire family gathered after supper, their hearts heavy with fear, confusion, and sadness. They were at a loss for what to do next. Suddenly, Murtadha approached Essam and reassured him, "I understand that neither you nor your son have any ties to ISIS. It is preposterous for someone with a doctorate to support such a group; the officer can confirm this and release your son within 30 minutes."

After a brief pause, Murtadha suggested, "What if I speak with the officer? Perhaps he would consider releasing your son in exchange for a sum of money." However, he made it clear that he would not accept any payment from them. He empathized with their situation, acknowledging that their son was innocent of any involvement with ISIS.

Israa prayed that God would keep Murtadha safe for his mom. Grant him success and give him what he desires.

Essam instructed him to enter negotiations with the man, emphasizing the importance of protecting their son.

Murtadha, feeling confident, approached the officer and calmly stated, "Sir, I'm certain the boy has no ties to ISIS." He waited for the officer's reaction before suggesting, "Why not just take a sum of money from them and let him go?"

The officer's response was unpleased, as he angrily questioned, "Are you attempting to bribe me, Murtadha?"

Murtadha quickly clarified, "No, sir, not a bribe; think of it as a fine for the father's excessive criticism of the government."

After some contemplation, the officer decided, "Fine, inform them they must pay twenty thousand dollars, and then they can leave with their son."

"Excuse me, good sir," Murtadha began, "but this poor family, I guess, has no more than $10,000 as they journey to Baghdad. They need food, shelter, and other expenses covered. If Your Excellency could kindly take $8,000 from them and graciously leave them with $2,000, or better yet, just let them go for free, that would be splendid; in my humble opinion, it's for my sake."

The officer raised an eyebrow and asked, "What's your deal with this family, Murtadha?"

Murtadha replied confidently, "There's no proof of their wrongdoing. It would be unfair to keep holding this child."

After some contemplation, the officer finally relented, saying, "Fine, we'll release him to you at no cost."

Murtadha expressed his gratitude to the officer and informed Essam of the good news.

In order to prevent any additional inconvenience at checkpoints, Murtadha promptly retrieved Arqam along with the required paperwork.

Israa silently prayed for Murtadha's well-being and success.

Essam, overwhelmed with gratitude, offered Murtadha his contact details, saying, "You saved my son's life. If you happen to be in Kirkuk, Erbil, or Duhok, feel free to reach out to me. I would be delighted to share with you some of the finest local delicacies from the region once Mosul became free."

Before the next officer's shift began, Murtadha warned Essam to leave the area promptly to avoid any potential re-arrest of Arqam. Essam bid farewell to Murtadha and sped off to Karbala in his car.

As the sun began to set, Essam's family finally made their grand entrance into Karbala. Essam, with his usual charm, suggested they visit a restaurant, satisfy their hunger, relax, pray, and then hit the road to Baghdad.

While seated at a table, the family captured the attention of Hassan, a man in his fifties who couldn't resist eavesdropping on their conversation. Their unfamiliar dialect gave a hint of the fact that they were outsiders. Curious, Hassan inquired, "Where are you folks from?"

Essam casually mentioned they hailed from Mosul City. Hassan, feeling generous, offered to foot the bill and even invited them to stay at his house for the night to recharge before continuing their journey. However, Essam had to decline, citing their urgent need to get to Baghdad ASAP.

When the bill arrived, Hassan noticed it was blank; instead, he found this phrase: "They are guests at the restaurant." Refusing to let them leave, Hassan insisted they stay the night at his house for some much-needed rest. His family showered them with an array of snacks and treats, showing off their hospitality.

After a night of rest, Essam's family bid farewell the next morning after breakfast, bellies full and ready to tackle the road to Baghdad.

Essam placed a call to Dr. Abbas, a colleague from the University of Baghdad who frequently visits him in Mosul. Dr. Abbas warmly greeted Essam and expressed his concern for his well-being. "Please reassure me. Can you tell me where you are currently?"

"We're now in Baghdad, and we're heading toward your home," Essam replied.

"Your presence made me feel happy." Dr. Abbas welcomed them warmly and said he was looking forward to their visit to his home. He warmly welcomed Essam and his family upon their arrival, embracing Essam with great longing.

"What delayed your departure, Essam?" Dr. Abbas asked, "Have I not often advised you to leave and join us?"

"There were inherent risks on the pathway itself," Essam answered. "In a fortunate turn of events, we narrowly escaped a potential catastrophe, and Arqam got out of prison miraculously." Furthermore, he stated that the conditions had become intolerable in Mosul."

Nisreen, the wife of Dr. Abbas, cordially welcomed Essam and his family upon their arrival; she sprinkled chocolate on their heads and ushered them inside, promptly commencing the preparation of lunch.

Dr. Abbas informed Essam that he would arrange an appointment for him at the University of Baghdad and expressed his desire for Essam to stay with him. Furthermore, he extended a warm invitation for Essam and his family to reside in the annex next to his main residence until the resolution of these difficulties."

Essam expressed gratitude for the amicable salutation and said, "The University of Mosul established a branch in Kirkuk; I have received multiple phone calls from university personnel inquiring about individuals with scholarly expertise, so I am required to travel to Kirkuk to re-establish teaching and join my students."

Dr. Abbas recommended that "you stay here for a few days to take a break from the challenges of traveling and share with me the events that have occurred during your journey. This will allow you and your family to relax and unwind before continuing on your travels."

"We'll stay here tonight." Essam stated "I got a little sleep for a few days. I will rest until lunchtime tomorrow, and then we have to leave because I fear they will not allow me to participate in my work if I am late. You will certainly learn about the entire story from your wife; I think women wait until they finish telling the whole story before going to bed."

Dr. Abbas had a similar view, saying, "I believe you are right; I will hear all about it from my wife."

Then he tried to call his friend Arsen in Kirkuk and asked him to find a rental house for Dr. Essam, as he wanted to leave for Kirkuk tomorrow.

"Please think I am the one who comes to you," Abbas said to Arsan.

"You just order, and I will carry out it, but for your information, almost every house in Kirkuk has an occupant. It can be difficult to find a rental home in a good location because of the large number of displaced people. In the meantime, I can always welcome them to remain my guests." Arsen replied.

Israa spent the entire night recounting to Nisreen and her daughters the challenges they had overcome and the dangers they had encountered.

"Wow, Nisreen, what a brilliant idea! This tale has all the makings of a hit Mexican series."

Israa exclaimed, bursting into laughter. Thanks to Nisreen's suggestion and their miraculous rescue, Israa could not contain her joy and simply had to agree, "You're right." It looks like we have the next big telenovela in our hands, folks."

When Essam arrived in Kirkuk, he apologized to Arsen for staying with him, thanked him for his generous offer, and said he would rather wait in a hotel until he finds a house to rent.

They searched everywhere for a while before settling on a motel with two rooms for $1,000 a month. They spent a total of two months there. Then they moved to a house, where they stayed until the liberation of Mosul.

During his college enrollment, Essam was busy, but he remembered Layla's letter to Fouad a few days after his arrival. Then he called Fouad and said, "I have a letter for you."

He certainly knew it was from Layla, so Fouad inquired about his address. Then he picked up the letter and opened it to read its contents. What did Layla's message to Fouad include?

9
Layla's Family is Planning to Escape to Turkey

Fouad opened the letter and found the following:

"Oh, my love, I know that your constant concern for us consumes every moment of your time. My fears for you weigh heavily on my soul. I hope that you will continue your studies with sustained dedication to achieve great success, and that you will not allow the specter of my distance from you to cast a dark shadow over your noble endeavors. Do not let the threads of fear tangle around your heart and mind; in your toil lies the real goal. Do not let the sad stories of our intertwined destinies influence you. Your fear for me is but a specter, a ghost that should not hinder you in your pursuit of greatness and prestige. A harbinger stirs in my heart, whispering of a day not far off when our paths will meet again. I do not say goodbye, for farewell is a word that carries the weight of separation and sadness." Good luck and great success to you!"

He saw traces of water droplets on the leaf, and he knew they were Layla's tears. Fouad pressed a deep kiss on the wet spots on the letter and exclaimed, "I caught a whiff of Layla's fresh scent.

*****

The government army, along with coalition forces, strategically encircled Mosul from three directions in an effort to liberate the city. As time passed, the suffering of the people intensified, with resources becoming scarce and prices soaring.

In order to assess the prices of the remaining materials, it is crucial to understand the initial costs; for example, the price of a liter of cooking oil can vary between \$30 and \$50, and the price of a kilo of rice can range from \$10 to \$20. Obtaining these essential items proved to be a major obstacle, even for individuals with financial resources.

The situation worsened when the government cut off electricity in areas controlled by ISIS, leading to a severe shortage of electricity and water. Some residents resorted to installing generators and digging wells in their backyards for communal use.

Both the government and ISIS imposed restrictions on the transfer of money, supplies, and fuel into ISIS-controlled territory, creating a thriving black market. In these areas, roadblocks and patrols increased, making it nearly impossible for people to leave. ISIS prevented residents from fleeing by using them as human shields and potential recruits, taking advantage of their desperate financial situations.

Within ISIS-controlled regions, only members and their supporters received food and drink.

Government checkpoints began apprehending young individuals attempting to cross into government-controlled areas from ISIS territory. Consequently, many fleeing individuals, including Layla and her family, sought refuge in Turkey via Syria. Harsh conditions had taken a toll on them, causing significant weight loss and a noticeable change in appearance. Layla's plea to her father resonated with the desperation that many people had felt: "We cannot survive here; our only option is to escape." This heartfelt cry captures the overwhelming sense of urgency and hopelessness that permeates their current situation.

"My daughter, do you not see how challenging, perilous, and costly the escape has become?" replied Othman. "And as you are aware, we do not have enough money."

"My mother and I will sell our gold and some of the house assets to aid in our escape," Layla said.

"Once again, my dear, it is not sufficient. Do you not see how the prices of gold and jewelry have plummeted due to everyone selling their gold? The smugglers are demanding large sums of money."

Upon discovering that most families in Mosul were struggling to make ends meet, Fouad sought out a person named Aiden who was working illegally to transfer funds.

"I wish to send $1,000 to Mosul," Fouad said.

"I am prepared, but it will cost you $200," replied Aiden.

"No problem; I am willing to pay," Fouad said, demonstrating his readiness.

He then contacted someone in Mosul and instructed, "Deliver $1,000 to the specified address."

Fouad handed over 1,200 dollars in cash without documents or guarantees. Engaging in this type of work is illegal; therefore, it is crucial for individuals to seek guidance from experts in order to protect themselves from falling prey to fraudulent activities.

Two days later, an unknown masked visitor arrived at Layla's house. Othman greeted the visitor at the door.

"Someone sent you a thousand dollars from Kirkuk." Layla knew that it was from Fouad.

When handing over the cash, these individuals conceal their faces out of fear that the recipient may identify them and inform ISIS members.

"Dad, this is a thousand dollars!" Layla exclaimed. "We will also sell our gold. We plan to drive to Syria, where we can sell our car, and then enter Turkey. Many people follow this route."

"Yes, Othman," Layla's mother chimed in. "If we remain here, we will starve, and Mosul will become a battleground; we must leave."

"Once we have acquired this sum of money, I am considering emigration as well," responded Othman.

Othman visited his friend Adel at his residence to inform him of his decision to leave the area under ISIS control.

"We are already prepared to escape," Adel stated. "Didn't I tell you about leaving two weeks ago, but you refused?"

"I didn't have enough money at that moment," Othman replied.

Adel remarked, "Why did you not inform me then that you were out of cash? I would have lent it to you." For your knowledge, Osama and I have planned to depart on Monday via a route that will avoid detection by ISIS if you want to join us."

Othman returned home to provide his family with an update after he agreed to accompany them.

They then embarked on what they referred to as "the path of perdition."

10
Layla and Her Family Embarked on a Path of Perdition

Late on Monday night, they departed the area using a dirt road in a minibus, accompanied by two hatchback vehicles. Their destination was a location southwest of Baaj town, near the Syrian border, which was under ISIS control. After taking a brief rest, they continued on their journey.

Adel alerted them to a checkpoint located approximately fifty kilometers inside the Syrian border; a friend had mentioned that they had been invited to stop, rest with the hostages, and have a meal at that checkpoint. However, upon their arrival, armed gunmen emerged and abducted several young individuals. Adel recommended that they maintain maximum speed in case checkpoint officials ask them to stop and rest with the hostages.

Upon crossing the border and reaching the checkpoint, the commander inquired, "Where are you headed?" Adel, who was leading the group, responded, "We are en route to the hospital in Raqqa City."

The leader instructed them to park their vehicles in the host's yard, enjoy the tasty meals, and take a break.

"It was more of a command," Adel remarked, as he was eager to pass the checkpoint and escape. Once they had all cleared the checkpoint, the drivers accelerated and sped away.

The control agents began firing at them. "Oh!" Othman cried out in pain.

"What's wrong?" Layla asked.

"My shoulder is in excruciating pain," Othman replied. When his hand reached over to his shoulder, he saw stains of blood on his hand. "I believe militants shot me," he stated.

Despite his injury to his left shoulder, Othman persevered and continued to drive. "Dad, please stop!" Layla and her mother pleaded. "Dad, STOP!" Layla shouted.

"If they catch us, it could mean the end for all of us," Othman warned, "especially since we evaded the checkpoint and are unsure of which faction it belongs to." After traveling approximately 35–40 kilometers, Othman's strength began to wane due to the bleeding, and he signaled to his companions to stop, although they were unaware of his injury at the time.

"Ha, Othman, what took place?"

"The militants shot my father!" Layla screamed in horror.

Osama swiftly entered his car and retrieved a bandage. As a paramedic at the hospital, he skillfully tended to the wound; his son, Bilal, took the wheel after carefully placing Othman in the back seat. Throughout the journey, Othman's moans filled the car, while Layla and her mother wept in distress.

When they arrived in Raqqa in the afternoon, they booked a hotel. Othman feared that the police would ask him who shot him and why, so he did not want to go to the hospital. He expressed concern that if they were to discover the truth, they might resort to extreme measures such as imprisonment or even death. He promised them that he would see a doctor when they arrived in Turkey.

Layla informed him that he could no longer endure the journey until they reached Turkey. There is not much time left. Groups that left a month earlier were unable to enter Turkey yet.

Othman expressed concern that both he and the group may face arrest. He emphasized his fear for the companions' safety and declared his willingness to sacrifice himself if necessary. Othman stated, "If I must die, I would prefer to be outside the hospital to protect you."

"I have antibiotics, bandages, and painkillers on hand, which should be sufficient for his needs. It is crucial to clean and sterilize the wound daily, especially now that the bleeding has stopped," Osama stated.

Othman initially felt better and began to eat. In addition, he sometimes left the hotel and walked around the neighborhood. However, six days later, his condition deteriorated considerably. Osama stated that he needed stronger antibiotics because he seemed to have septicemia. "I'll buy medications from the pharmacy," he said.

Although Osama continued to give him IV nutrients and stronger medications, his condition deteriorated, and he eventually died.

Emotion and tears streaming down the faces of both Layla and her mother consumed their strength. The tragic events that unfolded only served to further break Layla's already fragile heart. Despite her immense pain from the bitter separation, she clung to hope as she reluctantly departed Mosul, looking forward to their eventual reunion. However, tragedy struck once again when her beloved father passed away, casting a dark shadow over what was once a vibrant and happy atmosphere.

Layla's heart was once filled with joy and exuberance, but now a profound sense of sadness and hopelessness has taken its place. It is a reminder that devastating tragedies can shatter the strongest souls.

She had endured the calamities prophesied by the renowned Arab poet Zuhair bin Abi Salma.

There are three things that test one's patience and leave even the wisest mind in awe; Forced departure from a beloved homeland, losing a lover, and parting with friends.

Now mourning the loss of her father, Layla and her mother found themselves unable to escape their grief. They spent three days at a hotel after Othman's funeral, unable to shake the pain of missing their loved one.

Osama, Adel, and Layla decided to sell their cars at a significantly reduced price in order to raise funds for their next departure. They are now actively seeking a way for Turkey. After a day of searching, Adel found a smuggler willing to help them escape for $200 per person. The smuggler instructed them to prepare for their journey and provided them with sedative syrup to keep the babies quiet and avoid detection by ISIS agents.

Despite receiving food from comrades, Layla and her mother were not in the mood to eat. Layla either weeps uncontrollably or rests quietly when she feels overwhelmed or disoriented.

Then they departed, hidden inside a tanker.

11
Moving to the Region Controlled by the Free Syrian Army

Two days later, the smuggler shouted, "Prepare yourselves, prepare yourselves," as he knocked on the doors of the three households. "Let's move." Each person gathered his bags and belongings and followed the smuggler to a large water tank truck. The front third of the vehicle was empty, separated from the back two-thirds, which were filled with water. The smuggler opened a hatch door at the bottom of the truck and placed a small barrel underneath before instructing, "Climb into the tank."

One by one, the three families crouched down and entered the tank through the hatch door. The smuggler sealed the door, leaving small cracks for ventilation. Layla expressed her discomfort, feeling suffocated and claustrophobic. She questioned how long they would be in this confined space. Adel reassured her, promising they would only be there for a few hours.

As Layla memorized her father's death, her separation from Fouad, and the dangerous journey ahead, she wept. Osama encouraged her to be patient, reminding her that their struggles were part of their destiny. Layla struggled to find the strength to bear the burden, expressing her feelings with an overwhelmed mind.

Osama offered himself and Adel as father figures in place of her deceased father. Layla tearfully shared her father's wish to attend her wedding before his passing. Her mother, unable to speak, also wept silently. Suddenly, the vehicle stopped, and a voice demanded to know their destination and what they had placed in the tank.

The driver replied, "There is water in the tank, and I am going to Azaz."

The control official instructed the driver to pull over and wait on the side of the road until an officer arrived to inspect the truck. The driver waited patiently, while the inspector was delayed by twenty minutes. Layla and her companions felt anxious in the cramped and stuffy space, as the limited ventilation provided by the small holes was not sufficient. When the inspector finally arrived, he began tapping on the tank with his fist, causing those inside to worry that he would discover their hiding spot.

To divert the inspector's attention, the driver approached him with a cold orange juice, engaging him in conversation about the challenges of his job transporting water and his meager income. The driver even managed to make the inspector laugh with a few jokes. Eventually, the inspector signaled for the driver to proceed, much to the relief of everyone inside the tank.

After safely crossing, the driver opened an opening toward the driver's cabin for fresh air to flow in, allowing them to breathe more easily.

After traveling for four hours, the truck came to a stop, and the driver popped the bottom-hole door. "Get down! We have arrived at Azaz, a city close to the Turkish border. Thank God that everyone is safe."

After a recent rain shower, water has pooled in low-lying areas of the streets, creating muddy conditions on some unpaved side roads. Light raindrops continue to fall, adding to the dampness of the surroundings.

"Where shall we go?" Osama asked. "We have no local knowledge."

The driver asked them to follow him, and he brought them to a three-story building standing in front of them. There are numerous other flats in this area in addition to these rental units.

Each family occupied a room in the building. Following the placement of their belongings, Adel asked Osama to accompany him to purchase food from the restaurant for lunch, bread, vegetables, fruit, eggs, and dairy products for dinner and breakfast, as well as a SIM card for calling.

"Please, uncle Osama," Layla pleaded, "could you buy a SIM card for us too?"

"My dear daughter," Osama replied, "I will purchase a SIM card, and we will all use it."

Layla's sorrow only adds to her beauty and radiance. It is truly heartbreaking to witness her suffering. How can such a gentle soul endure the hardships that would break even the strongest of individuals? How does she bear such immense sadness and burdens? She brings tears to stone.

Osama and Adel returned from shopping with plenty of food.

"Uncle Osama, did you remember to pack a SIM card?" Layla inquired.

"First, have something to eat," he insisted, "then you can call whoever you like; it's been a whole day since you've eaten anything."

"Who in my position could even think of food?" Layla responded. "I am so overwhelmed by oppression and sadness that I feel completely full and have no appetite."

Layla's mother interjected, "My dear daughter, you lost a significant amount of weight in Mosul due to a lack of food. You haven't eaten anything today. I won't eat until you do." After a few bites, Layla got up.

"Uncle Osama, could you please pass me the phone?" she politely requested before dialing Fouad's number. Upon hearing only sobs on the other end, Fouad asked, "Who is this? What do you need? Why are you crying?" No response came. "Hello? This unknown number has caught me off guard," he said, puzzled. "What do you want? Who are you?" Fouad heard nothing but weeping on the other end. After ending the call, Fouad remained confused. The number wasn't Iraqi. What does this person want from me? Has something terrible happened to Layla? How did Layla get this strange number? Fouad wondered.

"What happened to the boy now?" Layla's mother shouted. "You made him puzzled. Osama, give him another call. I need to talk to him about it."

"Hello, may I ask who I am speaking with?" Fouad inquired.

"Hello Fouad, this is Layla's mother," she said, her voice filled with emotion.

"Hello, my mother-in-law? It's so good to hear from you," Fouad replied. "But why are you crying? Did Layla call me, and all I heard was crying?"

"Yes," Layla's mother confirmed.

"What's wrong? Why are you crying? How is my father-in-law, Othman?" Fouad inquired.

Through tears, Layla's mother replied, "He passed away."

"How did he pass?" Fouad asked.

"It's a long story. I'll explain when we see each other."

"Where are you now?" Fouad questioned. "This unfamiliar number is not an Iraqi number."

"We are in Syria, trying to make our way to Turkey."

Fouad urged them to call him when they cross Turkey to send them a plane ticket to Erbil, and he would come to pick them up from Erbil airport.

"How is Layla?" he asked.

"What do you think of a situation where a daughter loses her father?"

When Layla started crying loudly, her mother whispered, "Goodbye."

After two days of rest, Osama and Adel visited the building owner. They pleaded, "We need a smuggler to help us cross the borders to Turkey."

"The smugglers gave books three weeks in advance, and sometimes even a month or more ahead." The apartment owner said. "A large number of individuals are attempting to enter Turkey through the border."

Osama explained, "There is a girl with us who is in a difficult situation; after the tragic loss of her father while passing through Syria, she now remained with her younger sibling and mother alone. I am seeking your assistance in recommending a reliable smuggler with an upcoming departure date."

The landlord mentioned that he would try to connect them with his brother, who is smuggling, to place them in a transit group that is very close by.

Throughout the day, Fouad tried calling Layla multiple times, but she was unable to answer. When she finally picked up the phone, she was in tears and unable to speak.

Upon their return from the market, the apartment owner greeted Osama and Adel, who had been waiting for them. He informed them that his brother had arranged for them to cross into Turkey for $600 per person within a week. After expressing their gratitude, Osama went to inform the rest of his group.

How did they pass the steep valley?

12
TRANSIT TO TURKEY

One week later, a shouting sound outside startled the three families: "Hurry up and get ready! We are crossing the border tonight." He was a smuggler.

Quickly gathering their belongings, they made their way outside to find a small truck with a double cabin waiting for them. After thirty minutes of driving, the smuggler brought them to a halt.

After After a long walk through the spring landscape, with gentle breezes and lush greenery teeming with various plants and colorful roses, the group found themselves surrounded by a picturesque scene that would typically soothe the soul on a nature hike. However, fatigue and fear clouded their ability to fully appreciate the beauty before them. They arrived at the house to rest and rejuvenate. Layla fell asleep, while the others quickly followed suit. Each family found their own room to settle into. As heavy rain poured outside, water started to seep through the roof. Layla's mother sprang into action, grabbing three large pots to catch the water dripping from three different spots. Once the pots were in place, she returned to her slumber.

Layla wakes up briefly at the sound of water droplets hitting the pots, only to drift back to sleep, convinced she was dreaming. When one of the pots overflowed, the dros started splashing water onto her face, and she jolted awake. She sat up and noticed the water leaking from the ceiling. All three pots were full; she emptied them, placed them back under the leaks, and settled back down to doze off.

Four hours post-sunset, the smuggler's dulcet tones graced their ears as he commanded, prompting them to embark on foot. He kindly reminded them to maintain silence to prevent any unnecessary noise, and he advised them to strictly forbid smoking. The valley they ventured into is remarkably profound, with a steep descent. He advised them to progress down in a leisurely manner while maintaining a seated position. He stated, "Anyone who skates will end up in the water, and if the luggage falls or slips, you should not attempt to grasp it because you will fall with it."

After walking for thirty minutes, they arrived at the valley's slope. They settled down and started to drop quietly. Layla felt uneasy while sitting and decided to stand up and descend slowly. As she stepped on a rock, it slipped from under her leg, causing her to fall and slide, losing one of her shoes in the process. A large rock blocked her path, forcing her to stop after a few meters. As she reached for the rock, she noticed her purse lying on top of it. However, they were unable to find her lost shoes. Her cries for help echoed through the area, alerting the smuggler, who rushed to her aid. Then he found Layla sitting with tears streaming down her face, her mother comforting her. She explained, "My hip hurts, and my right shoe is missing." The smuggler pulled out four pairs of socks from his bag, instructed her mother to put them on her right foot to protect her from rocks and thorns, and he carried one of her bags. She agreed to take a painkiller that the smuggler gave her in order to ease her pain, and she began to descend slowly into a sitting position.

Layla muttered to her mother about the unbearable pain she was in as they crossed the valley. Despite the weight of their backpacks and suitcases, they had trekked up and down the valley for four hours.

Even without their belongings, they realized that crossing the valley would have been impossible due to their weakened state from a lack of nutrition. However, fear and the will to survive can give a person strength and endurance in situations they wouldn't normally have.

Approaching the smuggler, she asked for a brief rest, to which he replied that they only had two hours left to walk to a small Turkish hamlet where they could rest. Layla, exhausted, began to stumble like a drunken sailor, swaying from side to side. Adel, seeing her struggle, took her backpack and carried it for her, allowing her to continue on.

Upon reaching the village, the smuggler led them to an empty house where they could rest. He informed them that a bus would arrive in a few hours to take them to their destination, bringing them some much-needed relief.

An hour later, a loud knock echoed through the house door, catching the attention of Osama, who opened the door carefully. There were two police cars parked, and several police officers were in front of the door.

One of the officers inquired, in Turkish, about their identities and the reason for their visit. Confused and overwhelmed, Osama struggled to understand the situation. In a state of panic, he immediately reached out to Adel for assistance.

"Please come here; you are Turkmen, and you understand them."

"Yes, sir," Adel answered in Turkish.

The officer inquired, "May I know your identity and reason for being present here?"

"We are Iraqi refugees who have fled from an area controlled by ISIS in anticipation of the impending war."

The officer clarified that, as a result of the recent surge in individuals entering Turkey, crossing the border is currently prohibited. He expressed concerns about the potential presence of terrorists among the large crowds at the border. The officer informed Adel that an army vehicle would be arriving shortly to transport them back to the border with Syria.

Adel, who was visibly distressed, revealed that he is of Turkmen descent and is currently accompanying a young girl whose father tragically fell victim to unknown assailants. He emphasized that the girl and her mother are in desperate need of help.

The officer listened to Adel's plea, considered the situation, and then decided to hear from his companions and allow them to enter Turkey for humanitarian reasons.

"Where are they?" the officer inquired.

"In that room, sir," Adel replied.

The officer knocked on the door, and Layla opened it. Her weary expression conveyed a sense of despair and fatigue.

"This young girl is under terrible conditions, and because you are Turkmen, a bus will be arriving shortly to transport you to a facility within Turkey," he informed them.

The officer placed a call, and shortly after, a bus arrived to transport them to a seven-story building for temporary accommodation while entry procedures were finalized.

Each family occupied a separate apartment where they enjoyed three restaurant-quality meals daily, along with fresh fruits and candies.

Osama contacted Layla, as the Syrian phone network was still operating. "This is a call for you," he said.

Fouad, filled with worry and sleepless nights, asked her, "Where are you now, my darling Layla?"

"We have reached Turkey. They gave us a temporary residence in a big building." Layla replied,

"On which day should I schedule the plane for you?" Fouad inquired

"Please wait, Fouad. Let us not rush into things. We are uncertain about our departure from this location. I will contact you once we are prepared."

"My soul is now slightly more at ease," Fouad declared. "I grew weary from staying up late."

A week later, after calling out the names of the three families, the police officer informed them that their paperwork was complete and they were to follow him to his office. Once in the officer's room, he returned his or her papers and issued each individual a temporary ID. He then announced, "A government vehicle will depart for Ankara in one hour if you wish to travel there."

"My brother and cousin are currently residing in Ankara," Adel informed his companions. "We plan to stay with them until we secure a rental apartment."

Upon arriving in Ankara, they settled in with Emad, who is Adel's brother. Layla asked Emad to contact Fouad and arrange for their return plane tickets to Iraq. She emphasized the urgency of the matter.

Adel explained that they were unable to leave Turkey now due to their illegal entry; therefore, they needed to visit the Iraqi embassy to obtain a transit passport. Layla expressed her confusion about the process, as she was unfamiliar with the Turkish language and unsure of how to proceed.

Adel reassured her, advising her not to worry and promising to help her complete the necessary paperwork.

They were in a rush, so she expressed her gratitude and requested that he complete the task immediately. Adel explained that since tomorrow is Sunday, there will be no work hours. He assured her that he would accompany her, along with her mother and younger brother, the day after tomorrow. He also mentioned that it could take two to three months to obtain their transit passports.

"I have no more strength to bear this patience," she whispered, her voice filled with sorrow.

The news hit her like a thunderbolt, piercing her heart like an arrow. How will she handle being apart from Fouad for another three months? Especially in the absence of her father, as her funds dwindled and anxiety mounted, despair surrounded her as she contemplated the dangers ahead. However, she turned to God, seeking His help to ease her troubles and carry her heavy load.

Emad committed to informing the Iraqi embassy staff about her predicament and requesting their help. Tears streamed down her face as she struggled to comprehend how she would endure the prolonged separation from Fouad while grieving her father's sudden passing. She continued to speak to herself.

"Father, I used to find comfort in resting my head on your chest when I was feeling down; now, I am unable to visit your grave because it is located in a foreign land," she sobbed uncontrollably.

The following day, they found themselves waiting in line at the Iraqi embassy on Monday. When it was their turn, Emad addressed the employee. "This young girl currently resides with her mother and younger sibling. An unknown militant murdered her father on their journey here." Tears welled up in his eyes as he continued, "Their cries seem never-ending. Is it possible to expedite the passport process?"

The employee, upon seeing the distress in their faces, paused for a moment, pondered, and then replied, "You can return in two weeks to collect your passports. Does that work for you?"

With her mind racing about how she would manage to be away from Fouad for three months, Layla was relieved to learn that there would only be two weeks.

Adel and Osama were in search of apartments near Emad's home, and they successfully found and rented suitable ones. Their Turkish neighbors offered some valuable advice, cautioning them against making any purchases. They assured them that they would provide all the necessary furniture and supplies for their new homes, just as they had done for many other immigrants in the past.

"Why are you paying rent for an apartment if you're not staying here long-term?" Emad inquired of Layla, who was also looking to rent an apartment. He then kindly suggested, "My daughters consider you like a sister. You are welcome to stay with them until you depart for Iraq."

Layla expressed her gratitude for his hospitality and generosity. In addition, two weeks later, Layla received her family's passports. She then asked, "Uncle Emad, can I call Fouad?"

After a long separation, the two lovers meet once again.

13
LAYLA WAS BACK IN IRAQ

She contacted Fouad, who had been in daily communication with her and was up to date on all her news. Fouad asked if they had received their transit passports yet, to which Layla confirmed and requested that he book their tickets for the following day. Fouad responded that he would send the tickets via WhatsApp within an hour, adding, "My darling, consider it done and take it from my eyes."

After completing the necessary paperwork and enduring the waiting period, they finally boarded their flight for the first time together. Layla felt a mix of joy and sorrow. She was excited to reunite with Fouad after a long separation, but she was also grieving the recent loss of her father.

As Layla contemplated her conflicting emotions, the plane landed at Erbil International Airport. They disembarked, completed the necessary procedures, and retrieved their luggage. Layla spotted Fouad, hurried towards him, and stopped just 10 meters away.

Fouad glanced at her briefly before looking away, as if expecting someone else. Layla stood frozen, tears staining her cheeks. Why wasn't Fouad rushing to greet her? Who was he waiting for? These thoughts filled her with anger.

"Fouad," Layla called out, elongating the vowels, "are you waiting for someone else?" Her voice echoed loudly, capturing the attention of everyone nearby. Fouad turned towards her, his face brightening with recognition. "Layla, is that really you? He exclaimed. "How have you changed? Have you been sick? You appear to have lost a significant amount of weight."

Layla explained, "It was a lack of food, Fouad. For over two months, we survived by eating bulgur cooked in water without any oil added. We had to ration it, cooking small amounts at a time to avoid running out and going hungry." She then paused and added, "We were in Turkey for three weeks and managed to eat there. What if you had noticed our situation earlier?"

Fouad, moved by Layla's sorrow, tenderly kissed her on the forehead, consoling her. "Your pain is my pain," he whispered. "I pray that God blesses your father and grants you the strength and patience to endure."

He then consoled his mother-in-law for the loss of her spouse by kissing her hand. Thankful for their safety, Fouad decided to treat them to a tour of Erbil and visits to various shopping malls, culminating in a meal at one of the city's most renowned restaurants.

Although forgetfulness can be frustrating, there are instances where it can actually be beneficial. Layla's life would have been much darker if she had continued to mourn her father as intensely as she did in Syria and Turkey. However, as time passed, she gradually accepted the loss and was able to move forward with her life.

After spending a month in Kirkuk, Layla and her family began to discuss their plans for the future. Fouad asked Layla when they should schedule their wedding, to which she replied that they could do it whenever he wanted. They decided that a month later would be a suitable time, but Layla expressed that she had no desire for a big celebration.

Fouad understood her feelings, as he too had been mourning the recent loss of his father-in-law. Layla couldn't help but feel saddened by the fact that her father wouldn't be present to witness her wedding and that they wouldn't be able to have the celebration she had always envisioned. She started crying, but soon she composed herself and told Fouad that their joy would never be complete because her father was not there on their special day.

"Life is inherently unpredictable; every individual has a predestined end, and only God holds the key to eternity."

Despite the challenges they faced, Fouad and Layla began planning for their upcoming wedding and future home. But just seventeen days before the planned wedding, Fouad's father had a heart attack, resulting in the need for hospitalization and throwing off their plans.

Overwhelmed by Dr. Suhail's condition, they neglected to complete the necessary arrangements for their marriage. Layla, in her grief, whispered to herself, "Every time happiness comes my way, misfortune quickly follows. But I accept God's plan for me, hoping that our struggles will lead to blessings and beautiful children."

The doctors advised Fouad's father to avoid stress following his discharge from the hospital. Dr. Suhail urged Fouad to marry within a week, fearing he might not live to see the joy of his son's marriage. Despite Fouad's plea for more time, his father insisted on a quick wedding.

With a heavy heart, Fouad agreed to his father's wishes, prioritizing his father's health and happiness above all else.

As the wedding approached, Layla felt a fleeting sense of joy that quickly dissipated.

14
A Fleeting Moment of Joy is Experienced, Only to Vanish Swiftly

After a whirlwind week of last-minute preparations, the long-awaited wedding finally took place. The intimate gathering consisted of a simple supper for friends, family, and neighbors. To add a touch of rustic charm, Fouad's father took it upon himself to slaughter and prepare a cow for the occasion. The guests eagerly enjoyed the delicious grilled meat, and they generously shared a portion of it with neighbors and less fortunate individuals.

Fouad delivered a sermon to the participants. Expressing gratitude to the guests, he stated, "In deference to my late father-in-law, we refrained from hosting a wedding ceremony, and instead, we contributed the funds allocated for the event to the cancer treatment hospital." May fortune smile upon each and every one of you.

On his wedding day, Fouad placed a bouquet on his mother's bed and wrote, "You have always been the most beautiful and precious woman in my whole life."

Oh, how riveting it was to witness the profound moment when his mother laid eyes upon the bouquet of roses and read the heartfelt message inscribed upon them. With great enthusiasm, she seized the flowers, embraced them tightly, and inhaled the exquisite fragrance that undoubtedly surpassed any other scent she had ever encountered in her existence. It was truly a moment for the ages.

She retrieved the gift she had bought for his wedding day and started to write a heartfelt message. "You would remain forever more precious to my heart than my soul; yet if I could offer you years of my lifespan, I would give them willingly and happily, and my spirit would be content," she wrote with happy tears in her eyes.

On the day of his wedding, she had taken it for him. Fouad stooped and reverently kissed her both feet, proclaiming, "From this point on, we shall enter paradise."

After purchasing a unique wristwatch for his father, he wrote a heartfelt note: "Dear Dad, the one and only. If I could magically transfer your illness into my own body, I would do it in a heartbeat. I hope you stay well and continue to live for a long time. Cheers to you, great dad."

Layla was in the eleventh grade when ISIS invaded Mosul, disrupting her education and preventing her from completing her studies. Despite this setback, she devoted herself to caring for her family and children after getting married.

Layla and Fouad shared a deep bond, enjoying a luxurious honeymoon at a resort in Sulaymaniyah city. They explored the beautiful landscapes hand-in-hand, creating memories that would last a lifetime. As they watched the sunset over the mountains, they knew their love would only grow stronger each day. Their honeymoon marked the beginning of a life filled with laughter, love, and endless possibilities.

Fouad's father returned to the Coronary Care Unit after suffering a heart attack, just 53 days after Fouad's marriage. Concerned for his father's health, Fouad's mood shifted. Layla noticed his change and offered words of encouragement.

"Fouad, you are a strong and resilient man; don't let this situation break you. Your father will recover and rise again," she reassured him.

Fouad responded, "Oh, my dear, you have shattered me."

Confused, Layla asked, "When and how have I hurt you?"

Fouad explained, "During your time in Mosul and your trip to Turkey, I experienced extreme fatigue, nerve damage, and insomnia. I am at my breaking point."

Layla comforted him: "Don't worry, your nerves are fine. You just need to relax."

Fouad's father passed away six days after he entered the Critical Care Unit (CCU). This event crushed Fouad completely, and, as expected, his worst nightmares became a reality. This event cast a dark shadow on Lyla's life.

Alas, the fleeting nature of joy! Oh, the joy that did not last!

15
Severe Depressive Episode.

Fouad fell into a deep depression, cutting off communication with everyone, including Layla. His declining health forced him to put his university studies on hold. Despite Layla's efforts to engage him in conversation, make jokes, and offer guidance in hopes of bringing him back to his senses, her attempts were in vain.

Three months after Fouad's father passed away, Layla began experiencing symptoms like nausea and a rising body temperature. After visiting her doctor and undergoing tests, she received the surprising news that she was pregnant. Layla was thrilled at the idea of sharing this news with Fouad, as she believed it could potentially help him regain his former self.

Approaching Fouad with a sense of anticipation, Layla tried to surprise him with the news. "I have some wonderful news for you, Fouad," she sang out, repeating it several times as she swayed back and forth before him.

Fouad, with a cold tone, asked, "What is it?"

Layla playfully responded, "Can you guess what it is?"

Uninterested, Fouad replied, "I'm not in the mood for guessing."

Layla, trying to build up the excitement, said, "I believe you're smart enough to figure it out, my dear husband."

Fouad, with a hint of a smile, asked, "Did you buy me a new suit?"

Layla chuckled. "I'll get you a gift to celebrate, but that's not it."

Fouad then suggested, "Should we go on a trip to a beautiful place?"

Layla, beaming, replied, "I'm willing to take you anywhere you want, but the news is even bigger than that."

Fouad, now curious, asked, "I give up; what is it?"

Layla, unable to contain her excitement, exclaimed, "I'm pregnant, Fouad! We're going to have a baby!" Overwhelmed with emotion

Despite the joyful news, his expression remained solemn, devoid of any hint of happiness or a smile, as he asked, "Are we really going to have a child?"

"Indeed, the person who holds the utmost value and significance in my life is going to be a father," she said.

Fouad stood up and kissed her, a smile of joy spreading across his face as he began to repeat, "We are going to have a child, and I will soon be a father." A few hours later, Fouad began to cry.

"What's wrong, Fouad? Why are you upset? This is a time for celebration, not sorrow," Layla asked.

"Layla, I remembered my father," Fouad screamed, falling back into depression.

Layla tried everything to help him move on from his father's memory, but nothing seemed to work. She took him shopping and to popular tourist sites, but it was all in vain.

"Why won't you talk to me, Fouad? Where are the sweet words and jokes that used to make us laugh?" Layla pleaded. "We should consider seeing a psychiatrist to help you through this difficult time. What do you think?"

"I'm not crazy; I don't need a psychiatrist. I'm just sad about my father," Fouad replied.

Layla shared her own experience of losing her father and how she eventually found peace. She encouraged Fouad to try and move forward with his life.

Fouad explained that his time in Mosul and the journey to Turkey had left him sleep-deprived and damaged his nerves. He requested some time alone to heal.

"We should consider consulting a neurologist if you suspect nerve damage. My love, please don't hesitate to speak up!" She successfully persuaded him to schedule an appointment with a neurologist. Layla took charge and contacted the neurologist, providing a detailed account of Fouad's symptoms before scheduling an appointment.

Accompanying them on the visit was Fouad's mother, a retired doctor. The neurologist knew them through his friendship with the late Dr. Suhail.

After a thorough examination and review of Fouad's symptoms, the neurologist determined that his physical health was good, but his condition was more psychological in nature. However, he did diagnose Fouad with minimal nerve damage. "You should undergo a therapeutic regimen, including various tonics, to help restore and normalize your nerves," the doctor advised.

In a gesture of goodwill, the doctor refused payment for the examination, as it is a common medical ethic not to charge fellow doctors or their immediate family members. Fouad, feeling validated by the diagnosis, expressed his frustration to Layla. "I've always mentioned my nerve damage to you. Can you please acknowledge that?" he said.

Layla, showing her support, replied, "Your intelligence is invaluable to me. This home means nothing without you."

Fouad began his treatment regimen, with Layla actively participating in his care. Their conversations and banter brought a sense of normalcy and joy to their lives. Over the course of nine months, Layla showered Fouad with love and support, even while pregnant. She endured the pain of labor with Fouad's mother by her side, showing unwavering strength and dedication. She successfully delivered her baby, a boy.

Layla made a special request for her mother-in-law to stay hidden in another room, as she planned to surprise her husband with some news in the hopes of inspiring him to return to his usual self.

Her mother-in-law provided her with some helpful advice on how to help her husband regain his normal state.

Upon returning home, Layla found her husband resting peacefully in his favorite chair. She saw this as the perfect opportunity to try and bring him back to awareness, feeling hopeful about the outcome.

"Sweet Fouad, my dear husband," Layla said as she gently placed their newborn son in his arms.

"Do you have a name in mind for our son?" She asked with a warm smile.

Fouad responded by tenderly touching his son's nose and speaking softly to him before instructing Layla to lift him up.

It was a heartwarming moment when Fouad began to return to his usual self.

16
Horrific Accident

Layla positioned herself in front of him, swiftly removing the child from his lap and grasping his shirt. "Come back to reality, my love. I will never abandon you, even if I have to spend the rest of my days by your side like this," she declared, shaking him with determination.

"Why are you shaking me so violently? Please, step away from me," he responded with a touch of forcefulness.

"I will stand by you until you fully recover and return to your normal self," she retorted.

In a sudden burst of anger, he struck her on the cheek, causing her to fall to the ground. Tears welled up in her eyes as she rose to her feet, embracing Fouad and softly saying, "I want to see the hand that struck me." She kissed his palm and whispered, "Darb al Habeeb Zabeeb," meaning "Beating the beloved is a raisin."

Fouad wept bitterly as he gazed at her injured cheek. Overcome with remorse, he stood up, kissed her bloodied cheek, and apologized for hurting his beloved wife. "Please, hit my cheek until it bleeds," he implored her.

Instead, she tenderly touched his cheek. "How could I ever harm the face of my beloved spouse?

Realizing they had a child, he eagerly suggested naming him Othman. "Yes, my dear husband," she replied happily.

As Fouad gradually returned to his normal routine, a sense of relief washed over him, and he said, "Let's start a new life together, my love."

They went on to live happily, welcoming a daughter named Aisha 18 months later. Fouad was employed by the Kirkuk Directorate of Electricity after finishing his electrical engineering studies.

Three years after his recovery, Fouad accompanied his mother-in-law to Baghdad for medical treatment. During the journey, he wanted to lighten the mood by cracking jokes, including one about finding a man her age to marry her. However, his mother-in-law did not find the joke amusing and scolded him, though Fouad found it quite funny.

While driving on the Baghdad-Kirkuk highway, the driver hit a massive bump on the road, causing the car to flip and crash into a fence. The accident resulted in serious injuries to the driver's lower extremities, and sadly, Fouad's mother-in-law passed away soon after.

After careful consideration, the surgeon made the decision to amputate Fouad's right leg below the knee. A month later, doctors decided to amputate his second lower limb at the middle of the thigh.

Layla was overwhelmed with grief from losing her mother and seeing her husband suffer such severe injuries. She struggled to balance caring for her children at home with caring for her husband in the hospital.

Despite the challenges, Fouad's loyal friends stood by him, visiting him in the hospital and taking turns caring for him. They even prevented Fouad's mother from accompanying him, ensuring he received the best care until he returned home.

Success may bring new friends, but true companions reveal themselves in times of hardship. Despite the daily hospital visits, Layla managed to care for her children at home.

Oh, Layla, who could bear the burdens you carry? Her tragic tale, burdened with countless misfortunes and hardships from a young age, asks: How did a compassionate heart endure so many catastrophes yet remain unwavering and resilient in the face of adversity?

The world seemed to conspire against her, casting shadows of sorrow and despair on her path. The tragedies she endured, like a fragile flower battered by a relentless storm, left permanent scars on her spirit. After narrowly escaping one disaster, she found herself plunged into yet another. Her life seemed to be an unending series of misfortunes.

However, these adversities only served to strengthen her resolve and character, transforming her into a resilient individual capable of facing life's challenges head-on. Adversity, as they say, is a great teacher that cultivates greatness in individuals.

After Dr. Suhail's passing, his wife found herself living alone. Her son Fouad convinced her to move in with his family, though she was initially hesitant as her home held memories of her departed spouse. Eventually, she agreed and made the move.

Despite his injury and the amputation of his legs, Fouad managed to maintain his sense of humor and fun, bringing vitality and joy into the household. His positive attitude never faltered, even in the face of challenges. Fouad's resilience and ability to find humor in dark situations inspired those around him, bringing lightness and hope to all he encountered.

Unfortunately, due to his inactivity, Fouad gained weight and developed morbid obesity, diabetes, and high blood pressure.

Layla's dedication to her husband was a heavy burden for her to bear. Despite this, she never uttered a single complaint. Her face always radiated with love, happiness, and contentment as she served her husband.

Omar was thriving in his academic pursuits with exceptional success. Thanks to daily guidance from Fouad, Othman embarked on his primary education journey while Aishe was still a young child.

However, tragedy struck when Fouad suffered a stroke and fell unconscious. After spending several days in the hospital, he returned home. His right side was numb, and he began speaking incoherently.

Layla mourned her husband's declining health, shedding tears in private as she remembered him in his prime: youthful, elegant, tall, graceful, energetic, and happy. She made sure to hide her sorrow from him, knowing that seeing her in distress would only worsen his mental state. Despite the challenges, she continued caring for him.

Othman was in his third year of school when Fouad fell ill with a severe lung infection. Despite spending a week in the hospital, Fouad tragically passed away. Layla's tears flowed endlessly—a never-ending stream of grief.

In the midst of Fouad's illness, his mere presence brought solace to Layla's troubled soul. She found comfort and respite in caring for him, finding peace in his company during the storms that raged within her heart.

The weight of Fouad's sudden departure bore down on her, surpassing the grief she felt when her parents passed away. Alone in her dimly lit room, memories of Fouad flooded her mind—his infectious laughter, warm embrace, and unwavering support. There was a glaring wound in her heart from the abrupt emptiness that his absence had left behind. She sorely missed his voice and the warmth of his hand resting on her shoulder.

Amid her despair, tears cascaded down her face as she spoke with a trembling voice. "Oh, Fouad, you were the essence of my happiness and joy! My beloved, a kind soul, how could you leave me in this cruel world? Each day, I feel empty without you by my side. Your laughter used to fill the room with warmth and lighten my world. I ache for your comforting words and gentle touch. How can I continue without you?" She wept awhile and continued

"May God bless your soul, my darling. Since you left, the world has become a darker place. Since your departure, I find myself without another soul to lean on. The pain is unbearable, but I must endure it for the children who bear your name. Their innocent souls remind me of the love we shared, keeping me tethered to this tragic existence." With tears flowing down her face, she took a moment to collect herself before addressing her children and brother, who were crying, but she managed to find the courage to keep talking. "Despite the challenges I face, I find solace in my unwavering faith in God, who guides me through life's trials and supports me in raising my children and siblings to greatness.

Tragedies often act as catalysts for the emergence of extraordinary individuals, much like intense military training shapes fierce warriors.

A wealthy suitor approached her seeking marriage, but she declined, stating firmly, "I will never marry again after Fouad. My love for him endures beyond his death, and my focus remains on nurturing our children, who proudly carry his name."

Despite other suitors vying for her hand, she remained steadfast in her decision to prioritize her children and brother, finding solace in their care.

The longing for Mosul, her beloved hometown and Fouad's birthplace, remains a constant presence in her heart and mind."

17
Layla Visited the Destroyed City

The extensive destruction that had swept through Mosul upon her arrival shocked Layla. The city's buildings were in ruins, and the once lively streets were now eerily silent. Layla felt a deep sense of loss as she walked through the familiar yet unrecognizable city. The destruction was a stark reminder of the toll that war had taken on her beloved hometown.

As Layla gazed upon the destruction before her, it seemed as if she were viewing it with fresh eyes, wishing she had not borne witness to such devastation. The heartbreaking scenes unfolding in front of her stirred a cauldron of emotions within her, causing her chest to constrict with sorrow. Layla took in the ruins of countless homes and businesses, particularly in the heart of the city.

The relentless and indiscriminate bombing had destroyed every structure in its path, leaving homes, shops, mosques, and churches all in ruins. The streets of Mosul were littered with deep cracks and large holes, serving as a haunting reminder of the devastation that had ravaged the city. Amid the debris, the formerly lively city now rested in tranquility, with only the distant sirens' wails reverberating through the deserted streets. The displaced individuals roamed without purpose, their expressions marked by grief and disbelief at the devastation enveloping them. Yet, amidst the turmoil and desolation, a flicker of optimism persisted as they commenced the process of reconstructing their fractured lives and aspirations from the remnants of conflict.

She proceeded down the lane where they lived and stopped to look at Fouad's house, which had suffered damage from an explosion, leaving the door in ruins. Vivid memories came rushing back of the initial encounter with Fouad as she stood before the same door where they first met. As she stood there, she could not help but reminisce about the good times they had shared before the heartbreak of losing Fouad and his family took over.

She remembered the powerful verses of the renowned poet Imru al-Qais, whose words ignited like a blazing fire.

Let us take a moment to allow our tears to flow freely as we reminisce about the memories of love and home.

She stood before her home, the fence standing strong and the door securely locked despite the destruction within. As she gazed at the empty house, a wave of sadness washed over her.

She began to hum verses of poetry for Osam ibn Monquid.

I didn't love the house, save for its residents; peace is upon the house after they are gone.

If you're anything like me, you've lost loved ones;

or are filled with anguish and passion.

Stand at the dwellings of the departed and say, "O home, what have the days done to you?

Whoever—like me—has lost a love—don't hold it against him; words hurt.

I swear, I did not seek separation, but it was imposed upon me by those days.

As she stood before the door, a wave of silent thoughts flooded her mind: Would anyone answer if she knocked on the door? The people she held dear had disappeared, leaving behind a once lively home that now seemed empty and lifeless.

Under the rubble lay precious items and cherished memories that she longed to retrieve and hold onto forever. But the question remained: who would assist her in unearthing these treasures buried beneath the debris?

Tragedy and hardship filled Layla's life, leaving her exhausted both physically and emotionally. Despite the pain and despair she feels, she finds solace in memories of her husband, reminiscing about their younger days and the love they shared.

Their bond was strong, and even in the face of adversity, she held on to the sweetness and happiness they once knew.

However, her thoughts often drift to the traumatic events that have shaped her life. The memory of witnessing her father's injury, his passing, and the physical distance that now separates her from his grave all weigh heavily on her heart. Then there was the tragic accident that took her mother's life and left her husband severely injured.

Taking care of her family gave Layla strength, and in spite of these difficulties, she was committed to raising her son Othman, daughter Aisha, and brother Omar.

Omar's success in obtaining a degree that will allow him to pursue medical school fills her with pride. Aisha's bright future in elementary school and Othman's advancements in his education fill her with optimism for the days to come.

Through it all, Layla remains patient, persistent, and determined to make the most of the opportunities that come her way. She is a resilient woman, facing adversity with grace and courage and finding joy in the love and support of her family.

She came back to Kirkuk to live in the houses where the faint smell of her loved ones' perfume still hung in the air. Fouad's mother has aged and now needs someone to look after her.

Layla's first tale came to an end.